# THE DEATH OF
# EVOLUTION

## RESTORING FAITH AND WONDER
## IN A WORLD OF DOUBT

### JIM NELSON BLACK, PH.D.

**ZONDERVAN**®          A WORTHY BOOK

ZONDERVAN.com/
AUTHORTRACKER
*follow your favorite authors*

ZONDERVAN

*The Death of Evolution*
Copyright © 2010 by Jim Nelson Black

This title is also available as a Zondervan ebook.
Visit www.zondervan.com/ebooks.

This title is also available in a Zondervan audio edition.
Visit www.zondervan.fm.

Requests for information should be addressed to:
Zondervan, *Grand Rapids, Michigan 49530*

Library of Congress Cataloging-in-Publication Data

Black, Jim Nelson.
   The death of evolution: restoring faith & wonder in a world of doubt / Jim Nelson
Black.
      p. cm.
   "A publication of Worthy Media, Inc."
   ISBN 978-0-310-32745-5 (hardcover, jacketed)
   1. Apologetics. 2. Religion and science. 3. Evolution—Religious aspects—
Christianity. I. Title.
BT1220.B53   2010
231.7'652–dc22                                                     2010000122

Packaged by Worthy Media. For subsidiary and foreign rights contact
info@worthymedia.com.

Cover design: The DesignWorks Group
Cover illustration: Connie Gabbert
Interior design: Inside Out Design & Typesetting

Printed in the United States of America

10  11  12  13  14  15  /DCI/  16  15  14  13  12  11  10  9  8  7  6  5  4  3  2  1

# CONTENTS

# PREFACE

The title of this book, *The Death of Evolution*, is not a statement expressing a present reality but, rather, the prediction of an inevitable future. It was chosen in order to communicate two things: First, evolution as an explanation for life, the order of the cosmos, and the diversity of the species has never been viable. It is, and always has been, dead—dead to reason, dead to supporting evidence, and dead to common sense.

Second, while it's obvious that evolution as a theory is not literally dead as a prevailing belief in pop culture and among many in major academic and scientific institutions, it is losing steam as a more rational and viable alternative gains ground. If this trend continues, the death of evolution as a dominant theory looms somewhere on the horizon.

# PREFACE

Any theory that defies obvious reality so blatantly as evolution cannot long survive. It is a sandcastle sure to be washed away by the waves of truth already lapping at its foundation. Its death, while perhaps not immediately imminent, is nevertheless inevitable.

Thinking people, including a surprising number of biologists and natural scientists, are beginning to catch on to Darwin's contrived justifications for a theory—a theory that is misinformed and ill conceived. Here is just a sampling of their conclusions:

The spiritual worldview provides another way of finding truth. Scientists who deny this would be well advised to consider the limits of their own tools.

> —*Dr. Francis S. Collins, geneticist; director,*
> *National Institutes of Health*

We have not the slightest chance of a chemical evolutionary origin for even the simplest of cells.

> —*Dr. Dean H. Kenyon, professor emeritus of biology,*
> *San Francisco State University*

Darwinism is a trivial idea that has been elevated to the status of the scientific theory that governs modern biology.

> —*Dr. Michael Egnor, professor of neurosurgery and pediatrics,*
> *State University of New York, Stony Brook*

# PREFACE

The probability of life originating from accident is comparable to the probability of the unabridged dictionary resulting from an explosion in a printing shop.

*—Dr. Edwin Conklin, evolutionist; professor of biology,*
*Princeton University*

I am convinced . . . that Darwinism, in whatever form, is not in fact a scientific theory, but a pseudo-metaphysical hypothesis decked out in scientific garb. In reality the theory derives its support not from empirical data or logical deductions of a scientific kind but from the circumstance that it happens to be the only doctrine of biological origins that can be conceived with the constricted worldview to which a majority of scientists no doubt subscribe.

*—Dr. Wolfgang Smith, reentry physicist;*
*former professor of mathematics,*
*MIT and UCLA*

The irony is devastating. The main purpose of Darwinism was to drive every last trace of an incredible God from biology. But the theory replaces God with an even more incredible deity: omnipotent chance.

*—Dr. Theodore Roszak, professor emeritus of history,*
*California State University*

# PREFACE

Modern science is already, in a very serious sense, Christian. It germinated in and was nurtured by the Christian philosophy of creation, it was developed and established through the work of largely Christian pioneers, and it continues to draw Christians to its endeavors today.

> —*Dr. Ian Hutchinson, professor of nuclear engineering, MIT;*
> *fellow, the American Physical Society and the Institute of Physics*

As a scientist you grow to assume that science will answer everything and that religion is fictional. There are mysteries that science cannot explain . . . and divine inspiration may be a rational explanation.

> —*Dr. Andrew Parker, biologist,*
> *Oxford University*

More and more thinking people are waking up and turning away from Darwin's hypotheses. As this trend continues, this title—*The Death of Evolution*—will move from the predictive to the actual.

# ACKNOWLEDGMENTS

The author wishes to express sincere appreciation to Byron Williamson and Rob Birkhead of Worthy Media. Special thanks to Tom Williams for his always-stimulating creative input and editorial suggestions, and to Kris Bearss and Leslie Peterson for their stellar editorial skills. I am indebted also to John West, William Dembski, Stephen Meyer, Jay Richards, and Ray Bohlin of the Discovery Institute for sharing new and timely information regarding the science of Intelligent Design, and to Randy Isaac of the American Scientific Affiliation for additional research and information concerning the growing number of Christians in the scientific community. And, not least, warm thank you to my wife, Connee, for her support, and to my colleagues, Jim Underwood and Richard Westfall, for their unflagging friendship and good humor. Every one of them a blessing.

# INTRODUCTION

*To me, belief in a final cause, a Creator-God, gives a coherent understanding of why the universe seems so congenially designed for the existence of intelligent, self-reflective life.*

Dr. Owen Gingerich, emeritus astronomer,
Smithsonian Astrophysical Observatory[1]

You don't want to mess with the bombardier beetle. This innocuous-looking little bug is one of the most insidious creatures on the planet. Less than an inch long, nattily outfitted in its two-toned suit, this seemingly defenseless little deceiver appears to be tasty, easy prey for many small animals. But as a predator approaches, licking its chops, the beetle suddenly fires its secret James Bond weapon—a high-pressured jet of scalding, noxious liquid—into its attacker's face, sending the hapless animal scurrying away yelping in pain, wiser but still hungry.

The mechanisms that enable the bombardier beetle to fire that repelling stream are complex and amazing. When danger approaches, the beetle secretes hydrogen peroxide and hydroquinone into a storage chamber inside its body. By muscular tension, it then moves the chemicals to a compartment called the *explosion chamber*. At the moment of need, the beetle's body injects a triggering chemical into the explosion chamber, causing a boiling-hot, toxic liquid to spew out the beetle's rear end and into the face of its attacker.

Three separate chemicals and two chambers must exist simultaneously for this system to work. According to the theory of evolution, these chemicals and chambers and the mechanisms that operate them evolved over time. But this claim raises critical questions of logic: How could such an interdependent system of complex interrelated chemicals, chambers, and muscles have evolved by gradual steps? If that little bug needed this chemical weapon to survive, how did it manage to stay alive for millions of years while the complex mechanism was evolving? And if it did not need it to survive, why did it evolve? Even more to the point, how did all the chemicals and intricate mechanisms evolve separately when they served no survival function during the process of evolving?

As if these questions were not enough to discredit evolution, the theory goes on to claim that the bombardier beetle is merely one of the living organisms that resulted when life arose spontaneously from a "warm little pond" and over billions of years branched out into the million or more species known to exist today.

Evolutionary biologists have attempted to explain how the

functions of the bombardier beetle could have evolved, but those explanations range from the lame to the laughable. And this little bug is only one of an uncountable number of examples where evolution cannot offer satisfactory explanations for complex structures and functions.

## Nothing Comes from Nothing

The theory of evolution—or Darwinism, as it's known in its most widespread form—burst onto the scene in 1859 when the amateur naturalist Charles Darwin published his book *The Origin of Species.* While theories of evolution had been around for centuries, Darwin's book gave the hypothesis its current grip on the Western world. The theory, in a nutshell, asserts that life and the species were not created by a living, supernatural Creator, but came about through a series of blind chances. A bolt of lightning passed through a "warm little pond," as Darwin expressed it, and jolted inanimate cells to life.[2] These cells somehow managed to reproduce, acquiring more and more complexity in the process until they branched off into all the various life forms and over billions of years developed into the million or so species that inhabit our planet today. In other words, everything came from nothing.

Unfortunately for supporters of Darwin's hypothesis, the theory of evolution is dramatically at odds with the scientific principle described by the Second Law of Thermodynamics. This law, in layman's terms, holds that the total amount of energy in a physical system always decreases. It never increases. That means things can't wind themselves up; instead they run down. Things don't build themselves; they fall apart. Disorder continually increases.

Objects in a physical system cannot progress from disorder to order without the application of order from outside the system. In a physical system such as a running car, for example, the fuel in the tank will deplete to emptiness unless refilled by an agent from outside the system. This is considered to be one of the most basic laws of physics and tells us that no material object can by its own resources progress from simple to complex. Instead, just as hot objects get colder when the heat source is removed, all physical objects lose energy and deteriorate over time. A tennis ball will not bounce back up to the point from which you drop it—it loses energy with each bounce. If you keyboard gibberish into your computer, you will not get lucid prose on your screen. Garbage in, garbage out. And, as Julie Andrews sang in *The Sound of Music*, "Nothing comes from nothing. Nothing ever could."

We don't need science to confirm these facts for us; we know intuitively that things fall apart. We can see it for ourselves in the mirror after a hard day's night, or in the repair bills and maintenance fees we're occasionally asked to pay.

By asserting that humans arose unaided from a prebiotic soup, Darwinian evolution clearly violates the Second Law of

Thermodynamics. It tells us that order can occur from disorder, that life can evolve from death, and that awareness can emerge from oblivion. Even common sense tells us such things cannot happen and that evolution is nothing more than a modern myth. Evolution violates reason and at least this one foundational principle of science. But these facts have not stopped apologists for the myth of evolution from waging war on Christians and everyone else who doubts Darwin's hypothesis.

So why have scientists doggedly pushed this theory into the schools, colleges, and major institutions in spite of its fundamental contradictions, in spite of the fact that its basic tenets have never been proved? As we will see in these pages, evolution has become the necessary pillar to support a philosophy that is in opposition to belief in a supernatural God. By presenting the theory of evolution under the banner of science, nonbelievers think they can legitimize their agnosticism by propping it up with a theory that makes God unnecessary.

## No Apology for Faith

All this brings us to the central purpose of this book. Many believers today are uncomfortable holding to religious beliefs that have been labeled *antiscience*. Daunted by the prevalence of Darwin's theory in the schools, the media, and the popular culture, some people feel they ought to apologize for their faith in order to avoid being thought of as ignorant or naive by those who have swallowed the pop-culture line. This is unfortunate, because it robs them of the awe and wonder they ought to feel as beings who are "fearfully and wonderfully made" by a loving Creator.

Believers need not compromise, apologize, or hesitate in holding to their belief in God as Creator. In fact, we have ample reason to embrace that view with confidence. As we shall see, belief in God is not antiscience. Belief in Darwinism, on the other hand, is in opposition not only to belief in God but also to the principles of modern science. Darwinism is an anti-God philosophy offering no hope, no comfort, no happiness, and no ultimate meaning. It offers nothing but a cold, mechanistic existence in which man's only purpose is to live as long as he can before he vanishes into everlasting oblivion.

The repercussions of this outrageous speculation have troubled the world for the past 150 years, and debates between those who believe Darwin's theory and those who reject it have never been more intense than now. Thanks to a near monopoly on public education and rulings by the courts that no other theory of origins may even be discussed in the schools, millions of school children have grown up with this false interpretation of science. In fact, it's the only gospel allowed on public property.

But in spite of the dominance of the evolutionary hypothesis, a light is dawning on the horizon. The very fact that the proponents of evolution must resort to strong-arm tactics to quash opposition to the theory is a clear indication of its fatal weaknesses. A strong and viable theory should welcome debate, knowing that challenges could be met with reason. The ability of a theory to survive challenges is the essence of good science. But the power tactics of Darwinists make it obvious that they are running scared, afraid that public opposition will expose the soft underbelly of the hypothesis. Yet legitimate and highly persuasive alternatives to evolution are gaining momentum every day, drawing more and more prominent scientists into their camp. And believers have a growing number of influential allies.

## THE REVOLT AMONG SCIENTISTS

It is my hope that this book will inspire believers to hold with confidence their faith in God as Creator. It will provide a concise and easily approachable overview of the contest between Darwinian evolution and the new ideas emerging from science and philosophy about the authentic origins of life. Dozens of recent studies show that, despite the stranglehold of secular science on the origins debate, an overwhelming majority of Americans have not bought into Darwin's theory. Even though there are many ways of interpreting the Genesis account of creation—depending on whether one believes in a literal or figurative six-day period—the creation alternative has an enormous following worldwide. And that following is growing daily at a staggering pace.

Even more heartening, hundreds of scientists are now coming to the conclusion that the evolution hypothesis doesn't hold up—and some of them are speaking out. This is infuriating to the promoters of evolution. Books and articles keep flooding off the presses by authors like Richard Dawkins, Christopher Hitchens, and Sam Harris, blasting those who will not toe the evolutionary line. But, for all that, very few new converts are being persuaded to join Darwin's parade. In fact, they're marching the other way.

One reason for the reluctance of many people to swallow the Darwin line is the dark and uncompromising emptiness of the secular worldview. While fundamentalist atheists like Richard Dawkins angrily scribble away and grab every broadcast opportunity that comes along, no one is missing the fact that the theory they're pushing is a pretty dismal affair. In one of his books, mentioned later in these pages, Dawkins admitted that, "this is not a recipe for happiness. So long as DNA is passed on, it does not matter who or what gets hurt in the process." In much the same vein, Cornell University professor William Provine has been pitching the party line in public debates, saying that in the theory of evolution as Darwin conceived it, "There is no ultimate foundation for ethics, no ultimate meaning to life, and no free will for humans, either."[3] That says it all.

So which should we choose? Tragic hopelessness and suffering, no room for happiness, but the DNA is doing just fine, thank you very much? Or a world breathed into existence by an omniscient Creator who made the Earth a home of intricate complexity, beauty, and wonder for a teeming variety of life, including the humans he loves dearly and to whom he offers eternal ecstasy?

We realize, of course, that simple belief in God because he is more appealing than the evolutionary alternative does not mean our faith is necessarily true. We would be foolish to believe a beautiful lie just because it makes us feel good—which is, in fact, a charge that might be applied to the Darwinist elites. Rather, as this book will show, the alternative that offers happiness, hope, joy, and meaning also happens to be the most rational and defensible of the two alternatives—and it's also good science.

## SCIENCE AND COMMON SENSE

The fact is we need little more than common sense to tell us which alternative is true. This is well illustrated in a story about the great seventeenth-century scientist Sir Isaac Newton, who had a marvelous replica of the solar system sitting on a table in his laboratory. In the center of the device was a model of the sun, and spinning around it on thin metal rods were eight small globes representing all the known planets. The model was fitted with belts and pulleys so that the slightest touch would set the mechanism in motion. And it moved perfectly, just like the solar system.

One day a colleague who did not believe the Bible's account

of creation stopped by Newton's laboratory for a visit. When he spotted the model sitting there on a large table, he walked over for a closer look. He reached out and touched the metal rods and, like clockwork, the tiny planets began to move in well-oiled precision.

The visitor was delighted. "What a magnificent machine!" he exclaimed. "My dear Newton, you must tell me: who made this amazing contraption for you?"

Newton paused for a moment, then smiled and said, "Nobody."

"What?" the visitor exclaimed, shaking his head in disbelief. "Nobody, you say? How can that be?"

"Yes, that's right," Newton insisted. "The balls and belts and pulleys you see here came together entirely by accident, and by some unknown miracle they move along in perfect orbit just as you see them now."

At that point, the skeptic realized what Newton was saying. How foolish to think that a detailed model of the solar system could come together by accident. But how much more foolish to think that the earth, moon, and stars—and all of God's creation— could come into existence by mere chance. "Nothing comes from nothing." For thousands of years, since at least the time of Plato and Aristotle, around the fourth century BC, the great philosophers and men of science have believed that the precise motions and rhythms of the universe are marvelous beyond words—clearly the work of a super-intelligent Designer who must also be the Author of the order and balance we see.

Through the prophet Isaiah, the Creator declared:

> I am the LORD, who makes all things,
> Who stretches out the heavens all alone,
> Who spreads abroad the earth by Myself;
> Who frustrates the signs of the babblers,
> And drives diviners mad;
> Who turns wise men backward,
> And makes their knowledge foolishness.[4]

The universe we inhabit is truly a magnificent machine. There is very little dispute about that. The source of the conflict to be addressed in this book, however, is the effort of secular scientists and evolutionary atheists to rob the Creator who made this world of his glory, and to ascribe to blind chance the creative powers that God alone enjoys.

How unfortunate that some people are able to witness the order and balance of the universe and yet fail to recognize the hand of the Creator in his handiwork. And how sad for those who come to the end of life without knowing the Author of life in a personal way.

It's my hope that this book helps many people to avoid that

tragic end, and I also hope to show there is reason to rejoice in our faith—to see the glory of God in every sunrise and the love of God in the eyes of a child. This world is much, much more than just a precision machine; it's a place of unparalleled beauty and wonder. Once we rid ourselves of the doubts brought on by unbelieving philosophers wearing the mask of science, we can renew and solidify our faith in a great God who created the earth; populated it with the myriad life-forms that delight our senses; adorned it with mountains, valleys, rivers, and seas; and then gave this magnificent place to us as our home.

—Jim Nelson Black

# 1 EVOLUTION'S WAR WITH FAITH

*I myself am convinced that the theory of evolution, especially the extent to which it's been applied, will be one of the great jokes in the history books of the future. Posterity will marvel that so very flimsy and dubious an hypothesis could be accepted with the incredible credulity that it has.*

Malcolm Muggeridge,
British journalist and media personality [1]

Evolution's war against faith began with the publication of Darwin's book *The Origin of Species*, in which skeptics and atheists found theoretical scientific justification for their nontheistic beliefs. But for several decades the centuries-old alignment of science and faith, along with the obvious weaknesses of the new theory, kept the Darwinists largely at bay.

The first major shift occurred in 1925 when the American Civil Liberties Union (ACLU) was looking for a test case to challenge the Butler Act, a newly passed Tennessee law prohibiting the teaching of evolution in public schools. John Scopes, a high school coach in Dayton, Tennessee, responded to a newspaper ad looking for volunteers and offered to defy the law by affirming evolution while substitute teaching in a high school science classroom.

The Scopes trial drew worldwide attention when two heavy-hitting celebrities were conscripted to participate. Three-time presidential candidate William Jennings Bryan, a devout Christian, joined the prosecution team and noted trial attorney Clarence Darrow, an outspoken agnostic, joined the defense. While the state won the case and allowed the Butler Act to remain on the books until 1967, heavily biased reporting by the celebrity columnist H. L. Mencken gave the world a distorted picture of the trial, portraying it as a battle between ignorant religious fundamentalists and highly rational scientific principles. Mencken's distortions were then amplified and dramatized in Stanley Kramer's 1960 film *Inherit the Wind*, featuring superstars Spencer Tracy and Fredric March in the leading roles.

Mencken's reports and Kramer's movie moved the war between evolution and religious faith into the public arena and became footholds that enabled Darwinism to gain significant ground and eventually to take over the academic landscape. Today the theory so dominates our official institutions that you would think evolutionists have won and religious faith is in full retreat. Like Elijah fleeing for his life from the prophets of Baal, we're likely to wonder if only a few of us remain who still believe in the Creator God.

But in spite of surface appearances, evolution has not won the day. As this chapter will show, almost all of the prominent scientists of the past were believers in Jesus Christ who were convinced that true science could not advance without the underpinnings of faith. Even now the percentage of prominent believing scientists, while not a majority, is significant and growing rapidly as new discoveries continue to discredit evolution and validate the Intelligent Design (ID) hypothesis, discussed later in these pages.

As we will see in this chapter, while a majority of scientists still cling to the Darwinist model, by far the majority of Americans do not. Outside the insulated, peer-controlled towers of academia there is a commonsense resistance to the effort to embed the theory into the public psyche. As this chapter examines the barrage of words evolutionists have used to discredit religious belief, you will be heartened by the rational and faith-affirming responses of Christian scientists who refuse to sacrifice faith for fantasy. These scientists are convinced that faith is not in opposition to knowledge; rather, it advances knowledge. And the knowledge they are uncovering will advance your faith.

### THE SHAPE OF THE BATTLE

The theory of evolution as Charles Darwin described it in *The Origin of Species* is a cold and heartless affair. Random mutation, savage competition for food and mates, natural selection over billions of years, and only the fittest survive. Yet with the adoption of evolution as the reigning dogma by many of our most influential institutions, many religious people have accepted Darwin's ideas instead of belief in divine creation.

But the battle for the hearts and minds of civilized men and women isn't over just yet. With the growing importance of the ID movement, there is a strong scientific case for an alternative view. God has not been driven from the field, and debates between the rival factions are as heated as ever. As we enter the second decade of the twenty-first century, it's impossible to ignore the heated and often uncivil warfare being waged against creation by evolutionists. All of which makes one wonder: where is all this anger and invective coming from?

*As we enter the second decade of the twenty-first century, it's impossible to ignore the heated and often uncivil warfare being waged against creation by evolutionists.*

Bookstore displays are crowded with volumes from angry atheists: Richard Dawkins, Christopher Hitchens, Sam Harris, and Daniel C. Dennett are only the best known of a dozen or more who have written bestsellers in support of atheism and

Darwinian evolution. On the other side are eye-popping works by philosopher and former atheist Anthony Flew; the former head of the Human Genome Project, Dr. Francis Collins; former Berkeley law professor Phillip Johnson; and *Financial Times* editors John Micklethwait and Adrian Wooldridge, all declaring that faith in God is, indeed, alive and well.

According to a July 2009 survey by the Pew Research Center for the People and the Press and the American Association for the Advancement of Science, 87 percent of scientists believe that humans have evolved over time, while just 32 percent of Americans in general hold that view. And while 83 percent of the general public believe in God, the survey indicates that just one in three scientists would agree.[2] Other polls suggest that the number of scientists who believe in God has remained stable at around 40 percent for the past ninety years—since the first national poll of scientists on this question was conducted in 1916.[3] But the controversy is still raging and shows no signs of letting up.

For Richard Dawkins, the author of ten major works defending Darwinism and advancing an aggressively atheist creed, the fact that nearly half of all Americans (44 percent) believe God is the Author and Creator of life is tragic and profoundly disturbing. Equally troubling for the English author, 36 percent of poll respondents say they believe human life developed over millions of years, but that

# THE DEATH OF EVOLUTION

God guided the process. This means that a plurality of 80 percent of respondents to the Pew survey see the hand of God in creation while a mere 14 percent believe God had nothing to do with it. The remaining 6 percent are simply undecided.[4]

In his latest book, *The Greatest Show on Earth*, Dawkins reports on similar polls in Great Britain and other European countries showing that Christian faith in those places is nearly exhausted; yet Dawkins is deeply disappointed that a mere 48 percent of his fellow countrymen believe God played no role in the development of human life, while a plurality of 39 percent believe he did, and the remaining 12 percent say they simply don't know.[5]

## HARDWIRED FOR FAITH

For most of the last century, Darwinian evolution has been the only theory of origins presented in the nation's classrooms. School boards in the U.S., Canada, and the United Kingdom have consistently (and with legal backing) forbidden discussion of the weaknesses of Darwin's theory and likewise banned the teaching of creationism in any form. But as one British researcher reported, one-sided indoctrination may not be enough to change what children instinctively believe about God.

In a November 2008 broadcast appearance and public lecture, Dr. Justin Barrett, senior researcher at the University of Oxford's Centre for Anthropology and Mind, reported on studies showing that children tend to believe in God, regardless what they're taught in the classroom. "The preponderance of scientific evidence for the past ten years or so has shown that a lot more seems to be built into the natural development of children's minds than we once thought," he said, "including a predisposition to see the natural world as designed and purposeful and that some kind of intelligent being is behind that purpose."[6]

From studies with children ages twelve months to five years, Barrett discovered that by the age of four children understand that although some objects are made by humans, the natural world is different. As a result, he said, children are more likely to believe in creationism than evolution, despite what they may be told by parents or teachers.[7]

During a radio interview on London's BBC 4, Barrett said that anthropologists have found that in some cultures children believe in God even when religious teachings are withheld from them. "Children's normally and naturally developing minds make them prone to believe in divine creation and intelligent design. In contrast," he said, "evolution is unnatural for human minds; relatively difficult to believe."[8]

Needless to say, the scientist's conclusions provoked an outpouring of angry rebuttals in Britain and elsewhere. But Barrett isn't the only one making such claims. According to Dr. Paul Bloom, a psychologist at Yale University, our minds are finely tuned to believe in God. This happens, Bloom said, because some of the cognitive capacities that have made humans so successful as a species tend to create a predisposition for supernatural thinking. "There's now a lot of evidence," he said, "that some of the foundations for our religious beliefs are hard-wired."[9]

Dr. Olivera Petrovich of the University of Oxford found much the same things when she asked preschool children about the origins of natural objects such as plants and animals. She and her associates found that kids are seven times as likely to say the objects were made by God than by people. The responses are so strong, Petrovich said, that it's readily apparent that children have an innate concept of God, even without adult intervention: "They rely on their everyday experience of the physical world and construct the concept of God on the basis of this experience."[10]

In his most recent book, Richard Dawkins expressed shock and dismay that high school students in the U.S. and Great Britain often rebel against the teaching of evolution in the classroom. Citing a report from a group of public school teachers attending a conference at Emory University, he wrote that some students "burst into tears" when they're told they will be studying evolution. One teacher said her students shouted, "No!" when she began talking about the subject. And in another classroom, a student demanded to know why they were being forced to study evolution when it was "only a theory."[11]

# EVOLUTION'S WAR WITH FAITH

## Is Faith a Delusion?

This is precisely the sort of thing that drives defenders of nontheistic evolution crazy. At one point in the book *The Greatest Show on Earth*, Dawkins exclaimed that "history-deniers who doubt the fact of evolution are ignorant of biology" and believers in traditional creationism "are deluded to the point of perversity." He added that, "They are denying not only the facts of biology but those of physics, geology, cosmology, archaeology, history, and chemistry as well."[12]

On another occasion, Dawkins wrote that, "It is absolutely safe to say that if you meet somebody who claims not to believe in evolution, that person is ignorant, stupid, or insane."[13] Clearly his concern is not the sanctity of science but the defense of his own atheist worldview.

Adding fuel to the flames of controversy are books by Christopher Hitchens (*God Is Not Great*), Sam Harris (*The End of Faith*), and Daniel C. Dennett (*Darwin's Dangerous Idea*), each of which argues that traditional religious faith is everywhere in decline and belief in a Creator God is irrational and absurd. But for all their passion, the claims of the atheists fail the test of reality.

For Darwinists to call religious faith absurd is really incredible when you consider the faith of the evolutionist. Those who subscribe to the theory are logically committed to a number of scientific and philosophical assumptions completely lacking in evidence and defying rationality. Consider the magnitude of the leap of faith required to believe those assumptions.

According to the *World Book* at "NASA," there are more than one hundred billion galaxies in our universe, millions of which have been photographed using high-powered telescopes. The most distant galaxies are from ten billion to thirteen billion light years away. The smallest have fewer than a billion stars, while large galaxies may have more than a trillion, and each star may have numerous planets and thousands of asteroids or other astral bodies orbiting around them.

Our own solar system—including nine planets, fifty-four natural satellites, one thousand comets, and thousands of asteroids and meteoroids in precisely balanced orbit around the sun—sits near the edge of the Milky Way galaxy. This galaxy is approximately one hundred thousand light years in diameter and is estimated to contain up to four hundred billion stars. Our own sun is just one star in that system, and the earth is the only planet known to sustain living organisms with an environment suitable for human life.

The faith of the evolutionists requires that they believe all of this is an accident of time and chance. Furthermore, those who accept this view will also believe in the random, unplanned emergence of life on earth. The term *biological diversity* refers to the entire range of living organisms on this planet. To date, more than 1.75 million species of plants, animals, and microorganisms have been identified by science, and some biologists estimate that the total may actually be as high as one hundred million different species. All of this, according to the faith of the Darwinian evolutionist, is the result of fourteen billion years of random, unplanned, accidental processes.

But there is more. Biodiversity includes all the genetic variations within species—for example, breeds of dogs, varieties of roses, or coloration of moths—which are determined by differences in chromosomes, genes, and DNA. This diversity also includes vertebrates such as fishes, amphibians, reptiles, birds, and mammals, as well as more than 4.5 million invertebrate species lacking backbones, such as protozoans, roundworms, mollusks, and arthropods such as spiders, along with beetles and the remainder of the animal kingdom. These, too, Darwinists believe, came into existence by chance.

Animals, plants, microorganisms, living side by side in an equally diverse variety of natural ecosystems—forests, mountains, lakes, rivers and streams, fertile valleys and wetlands, vast prairies, scorching-hot deserts, polar ice caps and glacial ice fields, as well as lush, sprawling meadows ideally suited to the cultivation of crops. In each of these ecosystems, living creatures come together with humans, all of them dependent on the air, water, and earth that nature supplies. And according to the Darwinian faith, all are completely at random, without purpose, and entirely by accident—all having evolved from a single common ancestor.

# THE DEATH OF EVOLUTION

## JUST RIGHT FOR LIFE

Cosmologist Paul Davies, a popular science writer who questions many of the principles of evolutionary theory, further displayed the scope of the Darwinist's faith in his 2006 book *The Goldilocks Enigma: Why Is the Universe Just Right for Life?* As Davies explains, here and elsewhere, modern science has found that life on earth is not only rare but possibly unique in the universe due to the incredible fine-tuning required for its existence.[14] For example, one of the most basic requirements for life is the presence of water in liquid form. All known carbon-based life forms, including humans, must have water to survive. Water, made up of a precise combination of hydrogen and oxygen particles, transports the chemical nutrients required by plants and animals.

In addition, our seas, lakes, and rivers provide not only essential water vapors to cool the planet and regulate Earth's temperature, but are habitats for the millions of life forms that exist there and make up a large and important part of the food chain. To date there is no evidence that water exists in liquid form on any other planet.

We also know that the mixture of oxygen and nitrogen in Earth's atmosphere must be exact, within very narrow limits, for us to breathe. In order to sustain life, the planet must be precisely situated in the solar system to remain in the habitable zone around the sun. If the earth were to orbit just 5 percent closer to the sun, the seas, rivers, and lakes would evaporate and all carbon-based life would cease to exist. If the planet were 20 percent farther from the sun, the water would freeze.

Relative to the size of the planet, the outer crust of the earth is paper thin. If it were any thicker, the process of plate tectonics, which controls the inner temperature of the earth and the presence of chemical elements essential to life, could not take place. The terrestrial depth also affects the movement of molten elements beneath the surface of the earth, including the iron ore responsible for the magnetic field around our planet. The magnetic field, in turn, shields the planet from dangerous solar winds generated by the sun and keeps the earth in precisely the right orbit with relation to the sun, moon, and neighboring planets.

These are merely a few of the factors that make the earth just right for life. And there are many more. The moon, which is just one fourth the size of Earth, is the perfect size and distance from Earth to maintain the magnetic balance. The moon's orbit is precise, completing one circuit every twenty-four hours; in the process, its magnetic attraction controls the rising and falling tides of our oceans, seas, and major lakes. Meanwhile, the earth rotates on its axis, not straight up and down, but at an angle of 23.5 degrees, which is essential for the right balance of sun and shadow on the surface of the planet. The alignment and precise motions of the earth regulate the climates and the seasons of the year.

The chance of all these factors and the hundreds of others

that allow life to exist on earth occurring purely by chance are astronomical—the odds are literally trillions to one. The British mathematician Roger Penrose conducted a study of the probability of a universe capable of sustaining life occurring by chance and found the odds to be 1 in $10^{10^{123}}$ (expressed as 10 to the power of 10 to the power of 123). That is a mind-boggling number. According to probability theory, odds of 1 in $10^{50}$ represents "Zero Probability." But Dr. Penrose's calculations place the odds of life emerging as Darwin described it at more than a trillion trillion trillion times less likely than Zero.[15]

Yet Darwinists still believe the universe and everything in it came into existence not by design, not even by the intervention of a blind Watchmaker, but by blind chance and what the philosopher and mathematician David Berlinski calls "sheer dumb luck." In a provocative article in *Commentary* magazine, Berlinski described it this way:

> If the universe is for reasons of sheer dumb luck committed ultimately to a state of cosmic listlessness, it is also by sheer dumb luck that life first emerged on earth, the chemicals in the pre-biotic seas or soup illuminated and then invigorated by a fateful flash of lightning. . . . It is sheer dumb luck that alters the genetic message so that, from infernal nonsense, meaning for a moment emerges; and sheer dumb luck again that endows life with its opportunities, the

space of possibilities over which natural selection plays, sheer dumb luck creating the mammalian eye and the marsupial pouch, sheer dumb luck again endowing the elephant's sensitive nose with nerves and the orchid's translucent petal with blush.

Amazing. Sheer dumb luck.[16]

As Berlinski suggests here and elsewhere, to hold such a view is an act of faith far beyond anything expected of Christians or Jews. It demands a complete suspension of belief better suited to the readers of fairy tales. Yet the greatest danger of doctrinaire Darwinism is not the gullibility of those who choose to believe in myths; it is the moral vacuum that inevitably comes from holding such irrational beliefs.

### RELIGIOUS FAITH MAKES A COMEBACK

The abundance of evidence indicating an upsurge in religious belief prompted two English editors of the London-based periodical *Financial Times* to pen their newest collaboration, *God Is Back: How the Global Revival of Faith Is Changing the World*. In a comprehensive and compelling survey of the explosion of religious devotion around the world, the authors documented trends that are causing demographers and other observers of population dynamics to shake their heads.

"Almost everywhere you look," they wrote in the introduction to their book, "from the suburbs of Dallas to the slums of São

Paulo to the back streets of Bradford [UK], you can see religion returning to public life." The American model of faith—engaging believers in all aspects of their daily lives—is spreading throughout China and the rest of Asia, Africa, Arabia, and Latin America. "It is not just that religion is thriving in many modernizing countries," they said, "it is also that religion is succeeding in harnessing the tools of modernity to propagate its message."[17]

One recent survey of religious trends, they discovered, "suggests that the proportion of people attached to the world's four biggest religions—Christianity, Islam, Buddhism, and Hinduism—rose from 67 percent in 1900 to 73 percent in 2005, and may reach 80 percent by 2050."[18] But perhaps most galling to authors such as Dawkins, Hitchens, and Harris is the news, first reported in a June 2008 report from the Pew Forum on Religion and Public Life, that today's evangelicals are better educated, more affluent, and more engaged in their families and communities than other Americans.[19]

*"The universe has been created with intention and purpose, and . . . this belief does not interfere with the scientific enterprise."*

—Dr. Owen Gingerich, emeritus astronomer,

Smithsonian Astrophysical Observatory

Further, according to the same report, while 87 percent of atheists and agnostics indicate confidence in the Darwinian theory of evolution as a suitable explanation of the origins of life, 70 percent of evangelicals, 42 percent of those attending mainline churches, and 51 percent of members attending African-American churches reject those beliefs, preferring some version of the biblical account.[20]

In a 2007 book provocatively titled *The Dawkins Delusion*, Oxford biophysicist and theologian Alister McGrath, along with his wife, Joanna McGrath, penned a bold critique of what they portray as Dawkins' atheist fundamentalism and woefully superficial understanding of Christian theology. They point out that in the same year Dawkins published *The God Delusion*—claiming that no self-respecting scientist still supports the idea of creation—the distinguished Harvard astronomer Owen Gingerich published *God's Universe*, declaring that "the universe has been created with intention and purpose, and that this belief does not interfere with the scientific enterprise."[21]

Also in that year, Francis Collins, who led the Human Genome Project in mapping the twenty to twenty-five thousand genes that make up human DNA, and is now the newly confirmed head of the U.S. National Institutes of Health, published *The Language of God*, which contends that the wonder and awe-inspiring ordering of the universe declare the handiwork of the Creator, as the psalmist (see Ps. 19:1) and the apostle Paul (see Rom. 1:20) expressed it. Collins, who holds both PhD and MD degrees, identifies himself as a proponent of theistic evolution, which is the belief that God created the spark of life and established the laws of nature, but entrusted the expansion of the cosmos and life in all its forms to the engine of evolution, much as Darwin described it.[22] While this is not the traditional Christian view, it is still closer to it than Darwin would ever have accepted.

Cosmologist Paul Davies, mentioned earlier, said that the creation of life appears to be the goal of the universe. It is a powerful, self-directed, and irresistible force that "builds purpose into the workings of the cosmos at a fundamental level." Without rejecting Darwinism or claiming to believe in God, Davies wrote that the design of the earth is, well, miraculous: "not too hot and not too cold but just right."[23] This, too, while leaving many questions unanswered, is a step in the right direction.

What all of this tells us is that while the debate about origins and the nature of existence remains heated and unresolved for many, the claim that there is some uniformity of belief within the scientific community concerning the truth and reliability of Darwin's theory is clearly unrealistic and untrue. Furthermore, the fact that 150 years after publication of *The Origin of Species* there are still such profound questions about the science—and still so many conflicts among the evolutionists themselves—makes it more and more apparent that all is not well in Darwin's garden.

The theory of evolution is not in danger of disappearing anytime soon; Darwin's defenders are legion. But with all the fissures so apparent now in Darwin's theory, it seems evolutionary scientists would be willing to consider the importance of the interdependence of science and faith. One would think that objective scientists facing the weaknesses of their theories ought to display at least a basic interest in truth rather than resorting to name-calling and insults.

*The claim that there is some uniformity of belief within the scientific community concerning the truth and reliability of Darwin's theory is clearly unrealistic and untrue.*

### THE INCREASE OF FAITH-AFFIRMING SCIENTISTS

In fact, there is a growing number of scientists who have acknowledged the possibility of a closer relationship between science and faith in the new movement known as Intelligent Design. Specialists in this field, such as Dr. Michael Behe, author of the surprise bestseller *Darwin's Black Box*, speak of the "irreducible complexity" of living organisms—structures that cry out for some sort of logical explanation. According to Behe, the concept of evolution through "random mutation" and "natural selection" cannot adequately account for the complex biomolecular structures recently discovered by researchers using the newest generation of technological and chemical tools.[24] As the term *irreducible complexity* implies, many parts of an organism are meaningless without their corresponding complementary parts. This means that in complex structures such as the eye or the ear, one part cannot function unless all the corresponding components are simultaneously in place. And the components of a functioning structure could not possibly evolve into their present interdependent relationship because they have no intermediate survival purpose until all the components reach perfection and assemble themselves into an integrated whole.

But evolutionary theory has no answer for such a complex process. Because of the relatively unsophisticated state of laboratory science at the time, Charles Darwin had no inkling of such irreducibly complex mechanisms. He assumed that the smallest living tissue would be the single cell and even wrote at one point that if this assumption proved false his theory would be seriously undermined.[25] But what scientists like Behe have found is that the single cell is an incredible hive of activity with more than three billion moving parts and complex chemical reactions—comparable to a large factory working around the clock. A factory, the geneticist Michael Denton suggests, the size of London or New York.[26]

In his study, Dr. Behe showed how mechanisms such as blood clotting, the human immune system, the synthesis of nucleotides (which are among the building blocks of DNA), and the tiny propellers found on the surface of eukaryotic cells (known as cilia and flagella) could not possibly come into being through evolutionary means. In every case, there is irreducible complexity that cannot be explained by Darwinian principles. From this, Behe concluded that the complex biochemical systems contained within human anatomy were designed by an intelligent agent, whether it be God or some universal force.[27]

In countering Behe's challenge, Richard Dawkins has argued that biological mechanisms that give the impression of planning and intelligent design are simply illusions. As he wrote in the magazine *New Scientist*:

Darwinian natural selection can produce an uncanny illusion of design. An engineer would be hard put to decide whether a bird or a plane was the more aerodynamically elegant. So powerful is the illusion of design, it took humanity until the mid-19th century to realise that it is an illusion.[28]

This was, in fact, Darwin's view as well. But even to the uninitiated, such rationalizations must appear disingenuous and naive. The theory of evolution requires that we believe the opposite of what overwhelmingly appears to be true. The design of the human body, the miracle of conception, the interrelation of the five senses—the engineering of eyes, ears, nose, taste buds, and sense of touch—along with the mechanics of speech and the processing and storage of information within the brain . . . How can these things be merely illusions? Proponents of Intelligent Design hold that the logic, order, and complementary relationships of all the various parts of the design make a mockery of evolution. And the human body is but one aspect of our imponderably complex universe. ID holds further the idea that "time and chance" could never account for what we see around us.

For these and other reasons, many in the scientific community are beginning to express doubts about the validity of doctrinaire Darwinism. Some remain undecided about the Intelligent Designer while many others have come to the conclusion that the only explanation for the undeniable complexity and majesty of the cosmos is that it is the work of a super-human intellect. All of which suggests that now is a good time for an honest reassessment of Darwin's hypothesis and the problems it poses for men and women of faith.

## The Myth of Church Versus Science

The long and complicated relationship between the church and science is another area that has bred a great deal of discord and misinformation. Over the years, the struggles of the pioneers of modern astronomy—Nicolas Copernicus and Galileo Galilei—with certain officials of the Catholic church have been used as evidence of the hostility of Christianity to science. The saga has become a legend involving Pope Urban VIII and the notorious Cardinal Bellarmine. But the legend is largely false.

The late Carl Sagan, who was a well-known science popularizer and staunch critic of the Christian faith, repeatedly told his reading and viewing audiences that Galileo was unable to convince the Catholic hierarchy that there are mountains on the moon and that the planet Jupiter has moons of its own. Unable to deal with this scientific truth, Sagan said, the church tried to crush this brilliant man of science. But Sagan's version is simply wrong. In fact, when astronomers in the Roman College confirmed Galileo's observations themselves, they were thrilled and honored Galileo with a full day of ceremonies. While he was in Rome, Galileo received a hero's welcome from many church officials, including the pope. The majority of scholars in the church supported Galileo. The strongest opposition came, not from the church but from the secular establishment, who saw Galileo's work as a direct challenge to the theories of Aristotle that dominated scientific thought at that time.

Unfortunately, these facts have been largely ignored. And much the same can be said for Galileo's predecessor, Nicolas Copernicus, who was the first European astronomer to observe that the earth makes one complete revolution every twenty-four hours and that it completes one circuit around the sun each year.

Although Copernicus carefully confirmed these calculations, he was hesitant to announce the discovery and waited until the last year of his life, when he was seventy years old, before agreeing to publish his findings. Once again, when he did he received strong support and encouragement from officials in Rome. After listening to a lecture on the Copernican theory in 1533, Pope Clement VII was greatly impressed.

Sometime later, Cardinal Schönberg, a scholar who was an accomplished scientist in his own right, wrote to Copernicus, saying he had heard of the Polish mathematician's "having created a new theory of the universe according to which the Earth moves and the sun occupies the basic and central position. . . . Therefore, learned man," he wrote, "without wishing to be opportune, I beg you most emphatically to communicate your discovery to the learned world."

In the preface of his book, Copernicus acknowledged his indebtedness to the many friends and colleagues who had encouraged him to publish his findings—including Tiedeman Giese, bishop of Culm, whom he said, "spurred me on by added reproaches into publishing this book and letting come to light a work which I had kept hidden among my things for not merely nine years, but for almost four times nine years." When he dedicated the work to Pope Paul III, Copernicus affirmed his commitment to the faith. The Church had not buried his life's work but affirmed it, and helped to make it known.[29]

## FAITH BREEDS SERIOUS SCIENCE

There is no denying that both these scientists endured great struggles in breaking new ground; after all, they were introducing startling new facts about the earth and its place in the cosmos. Their discoveries were provocative and troubling to many, including some of the Protestant Reformers who, by some accounts, tried to block publication of their works for a time. But neither of these great precursors of modern science turned against the church or lost their faith in God because of it.[30]

The authentic history of science makes it clear that religion has played an important role in the emergence of modern science. Authentic Christian faith—following Christ's words in John 8:32, "You shall know the truth, and the truth shall make you free"—encourages the pursuit of knowledge that advances truth. Scientists such as Newton, Kepler, Boyle, Faraday, and Kelvin were ardent believers. Johannes Kepler claimed to be "thinking God's thoughts after Him." The scientist's pursuit of evidence through critical inquiry, rather than posing a threat to faith, actually enhances it by advancing knowledge and increasing our sense of awe and wonder for the majesty of God's world.

While many strident voices proclaim that no responsible scientist today believes in God, thousands of scientists beg to differ. As just one example, the American Scientific Affiliation (ASA), founded in 1941 as an organization of men and women in the sciences who share a common faith in God, boasts more than two thousand members, among them, Dr. Francis Collins and a long list of professors, researchers, and practitioners. For these men and women, ASA provides a forum for dialogue about their vocation and the life of faith.

*"Modern science is already, in a very serious sense, Christian. It germinated in and was nurtured by the Christian philosophy of creation, it was developed and established through the work of largely Christian pioneers, and it continues to draw Christians to its endeavors today."*

—Dr. Ian Hutchinson, professor of nuclear engineering, MIT; fellow, the American Physical Society and the Institute of Physics

Dr. Ian Hutchinson, who is a member of ASA, is a professor of nuclear engineering at MIT and fellow of the American Physical Society and of the Institute of Physics. His primary research interest is the magnetic confinement of plasmas—seeking to enable fusion reactions (the energy source of the stars) to be used for energy production. He also heads the Alcator Project, the largest university-based fusion research team in the nation.

Like many of his colleagues, Dr. Hutchinson believes that faith informs science by encouraging integrity and professional discipline, and by the knowledge that the laws governing the physical world were established by God and can be discovered through science. "Modern science," he said, "is already, in a very serious sense, Christian. It germinated in and was nurtured by the Christian philosophy of creation, it was developed and established through the work of largely Christian pioneers, and it continues to draw Christians to its endeavors today."[31]

During his journey to faith, Hutchinson discovered that Christians were pioneers in the revolutions that brought about our modern understanding of the world. "Any list of the giants of physical science," he said, "would include Copernicus, Galileo, Kepler, Boyle, Pascal, Newton, Faraday, and Maxwell, all of whom—despite denominational and doctrinal differences among them, and opposition that some experienced from church authorities—were deeply committed to Jesus Christ."[32]

Dr. Richard Bube, a former professor in the department of Materials Science and Engineering at Stanford University, served for many years as editor of the *ASA Journal* and authored many books and articles affirming the important relationships between science and faith. In one of them, he said:

The biblical doctrine of creation is one of the richest doctrines revealed to us by God. It reveals to us that the God who loves us is also the God who created us and all things; at once it establishes the relationship between the God of religious faith and the God of physical reality. . . . It is because of creation that we trust in the reality of a physical and moral structure to the universe, which we can explore as scientists and experience as persons. It is because of creation that we know that the universe and everything in it depends moment-by-moment upon the sustaining power and activity of God.[33]

Such comments stand in dramatic contrast to the claims of atheism and affirm the creative harmony of modern science and the Christian faith.

### CHRISTIAN SCIENCE IS GOOD SCIENCE

It would be easy to include testimonials from many others who have made the connection between what Sir Francis Bacon (one of the founders of modern science) called "the book of God's word" and "the book of God's works." But it should be obvious by now that a strong faith in God is not a handicap to rigorous scientific inquiry but a positive benefit. Dr. Henry F. Schaefer III, recognized as one of the world's most distinguished scientists, made that discovery as a young man and has never looked back.

A five-time nominee for the Nobel Prize, recipient of four prestigious awards from the American Chemical Society as well as the Centenary Award of London's Royal Society of Chemistry,

Dr. Schaefer has been a professor of chemistry at the University of California at Berkeley and at the University of Georgia. Along the way he has made many remarkable discoveries. In his book *Science and Christianity: Conflict or Coherence?* he talked about the most important one:

> From time to time, people actually do ask me, "What is your most important discovery?" And I respond that the most important discovery in my life occurred during my fourth year on the faculty at Berkeley. . . . At the time of this discovery, my students and I were doing some very interesting theoretical work on the identification of the interstellar molecules hydrogen isocyanide and protonated carbon monoxide. But the most important discovery of my life was my discovery of Jesus Christ.[34]

What made that discovery so important, Schaefer says, was learning that "the challenge to understand the riches of the Christian faith is quite comparable to that required to plumb the depths of molecular quantum mechanics. I've been at the former in earnest for a quarter century and haven't come close to exhausting the wealth of even 20th century intellectual writing."[35]

What can we learn from those, like Henry Schaefer, who have rejected the anger and invective of Dawkins, Hitchens, and the others and turned instead to the inexhaustible riches of faith in God? The answer seems to be that science and faith are not merely compatible but comparable in many ways, and ought to be inseparable. Together they open our minds to the grandeur of our world and promote the best kind of science.

For any scientist to dismiss the laws of nature and the objects of creation so clearly recognizable as the handiwork of God as nothing more than by-products of time and chance is to miss out on one of the most amazing gifts mankind has ever been given: the opportunity to unravel some of the greatest mysteries of all time. Surely this is the worst kind of science.

But as Richard Bube wrote, there is another alternative. "The Christian philosophy of science is this," he said. "Christian science is good science. And good science is science that is faithful to the structure of reality. Science that is honest, open, seeking to capture and to reflect the structure of the world that is really there—that is good science, and that is Christian science."[36]

Even if many in mainstream science have yet to come to that conclusion, there's reason to believe that things may be changing. In the meantime, there's a lot more to say about all these things. But first it will be helpful to take a look at the origins of Darwinian evolution to find out how we got to this point in the first place.

# 2 THE BIRTH OF THE EVOLUTION MYTH

*I am not satisfied that Darwin proved his point or that his influence in scientific and public thinking has been beneficial. . . . He fell back on speculative arguments. . . . But the facts and interpretations on which Darwin relied have now ceased to convince.*

> Dr. W. R. Thompson, entomologist; director,
> Commonwealth Institute of Biological Control[1]

A small spark in the wrong place at the wrong time can blaze into a raging inferno that can destroy entire cities or millions of acres of forest land. Legend has it that the great Chicago fire started when Mrs. O'Leary's cow kicked over a lantern into a pile of hay. The great Idaho-Montana forest fire of 1910 that killed eighty-six people, turned several days black as night, and destroyed three million acres of timber—equivalent to filling every car in a train twenty-four hundred miles long—was thought to have been caused by a spark from a steam locomotive.

The publication of Charles Darwin's book *The Origin of Species* was the spark that touched off a firestorm that has spread throughout the Western world and still rages today. Darwin did not create anything new with his theory: similar ideas about life's origins had been floating about since ancient times. But Darwin's book was dropped on the public at a time when the dry kindling of European rationalistic philosophy was ready for such a spark, and it ignited a firestorm that eventually swept across Europe and jumped the Atlantic to America.

How did such a phenomenon occur? Who was this man who lit the blaze? What factors shaped him and his ideas? What gave him a platform and motivated him to propose a theory that defied traditional Christianity and threatened to consume the faith of millions? How did this theory that stood against the religious beliefs of people on two continents catch on so quickly and come to dominate the thinking of leaders of the West's major institutions?

In this chapter we will take a closer look at the man who set off the evolutionary firestorm, to see what made him tick. Along the way we will refute some of the popular misinformation that has been perpetuated about his beliefs and motivations. You may be surprised to learn that this man, revered by atheists almost to the point of being their surrogate deity, had minimal scientific education, no scientific degree or credentials, borrowed much of his "original" theory from others, and stumbled his way into a prominent place in history. In fact, as we will see, his unsubstantiated theory was quickly dismissed as a fantasy by most of the scientific establishment and would probably have died in its crib had not outspoken atheists begun to promote it as an alternative to religious faith.

*Darwin's book was dropped on the public at a time when the dry kindling of European rationalistic philosophy was ready for such a spark, and it ignited a firestorm that eventually swept across Europe to America.*

### Who Was Charles Darwin?

No one would have suspected when Charles Darwin was born on February 12, 1809, in Shrewsbury, England, that one day the young man's fantastic ideas about the origins of life on earth would have such a dramatic impact on the world. He has been described as a very ordinary child who showed little promise in his early years and was a disappointment to his wealthy and highly accomplished father, the renowned surgeon, Dr. Robert Darwin.[2]

The fifth of six children, Charles was spoiled by his older siblings and doted on by his mother, Susannah, who was the daughter of the famous English porcelain manufacturer and abolitionist Josiah Wedgwood. Unfortunately, his mother's death when Charles was just eight years old left an indelible mark on the boy, which he masked by immersing himself in games and other outdoor activities, including long hikes in the English countryside where he could indulge his passion for collecting—insects, stones, bird eggs, and many other things.

To make matters worse for the boy, his father, who was profoundly disturbed by the death of Susannah, became reclusive and obsessed by work. He insisted that none of the children should ever mention the name of their mother again, which was especially devastating for Charles. Some biographers have speculated that this may have been the root of the illnesses—including frequent bouts of vomiting, nausea, and blinding headaches—that troubled him throughout his adult life.[3]

Even though Charles was a mediocre student at Shrewsbury School, his father was determined that his son would follow him into the medical profession, and used his connections to enroll Charles, at age sixteen, in the medical college at Edinburgh University—where both Robert and Charles' more famous grandfather, Erasmus Darwin, had studied. Before completing his second year, however, Charles knew he would never be a doctor. He couldn't stand the sight of blood and became violently ill after watching operations performed in the school's surgical theater.

Fearing that Charles was destined to be a failure, Robert Darwin reluctantly chose a lesser but still respectable career for the boy and sent him off to Christ College at Cambridge University, where he could study to become an Anglican minister. Here again Charles was a mediocre student and regularly skipped lectures. By cramming for exams for several weeks during his third and final year, he was able to earn his degree in theology, but he never took the matter further. He had no real interest in religion, no inclination to enter the priesthood, and he was never ordained.

## Darwin's Anti-Christian Heritage

For generations, the Darwin family had been outspoken religious skeptics. Although he died before Charles was born, his grandfather, Erasmus Darwin, was a brilliant and multitalented physician who lived and breathed the spirit of the European Enlightenment. He was a deist, highly critical of traditional Christian beliefs, and a political radical who never hesitated to say what he thought, no matter who might be offended. Erasmus had inherited a fortune and lived extravagantly. Eventually both Robert and Charles Darwin would inherit sizable fortunes as well, from Erasmus and from the estate of Josiah Wedgwood.

Charles' grandfather had no patience with Puritan morality. He fathered at least two illegitimate children but was praised as a radical and free thinker in the lecture halls and literary salons of

London and Paris, where he was well known as a poet, philosopher, and sage. As a member of the Lunar Society, which included many imminent scientists and inventors—including James Watt, the inventor of the steam engine; and Joseph Priestly, a radical theologian, chemist, and the discoverer of oxygen—Erasmus was welcomed among the most highly acclaimed intellectuals of his day. He was a friend of many of the best-known public figures, including Benjamin Franklin, with whom he maintained a long and cordial correspondence. The poet Samuel Taylor Coleridge, who found the elder Darwin's writings objectionable, nevertheless referred to him on one occasion as "the first literary character in Europe, and the most original-minded Man."

Today Erasmus Darwin is remembered as the author of *Zoönomia, or, The Laws of Organic Life,* published in two volumes in 1794 and 1796. In addition to lengthy discussions of then current medical knowledge, the book revealed the author's unconventional ideas about human and animal biology and a theory of evolutionary principles known as the "transmutation of human and animal species" that preceded Charles Darwin's *The Origin of Species* by more than sixty years. In the book, Erasmus Darwin described how living organisms may be transformed through biological stages, how sexual competition within a species affects natural selection and the survival of the fittest, and how higher forms of life have evolved from simpler ones.

These ideas, all highly controversial at the time, were spelled out further in his poem "The Temple of Nature." In it, Erasmus described how all of life originated in the sea, having evolved from a single common ancestor. All the changes we observe within the various species are due, he believed, to environmental factors.

## A Fateful Invitation

Like the grandfather he never knew, Charles Darwin grew to be tall and stocky and spoke with a slight stammer. He was generally quiet and shy, but what he lacked in social graces he made up for in his love of family and his addiction to outdoor sports such as horseback riding and shooting. He was an excellent shot and frequently rode into the nearby forests to hunt rabbits, wild fowl, and other game common in the area. According to one popular biography, Charles had "an insatiable desire to kill birds of any variety."[4] On many occasions he would arrive home after a successful hunt with a brace of game birds strapped to his saddle, ready to be cleaned, dressed, and prepared for dinner by the family cook.

While Charles continued collecting interesting rocks, fossils, butterflies, stuffed birds, and many other things throughout his time at Cambridge, he never seriously considered what sort of profession he would actually pursue. He loved the life of a wealthy country gentleman: entertaining, enjoying good foods and wines with friends and family, hunting with his dogs in the countryside, and managing his ever-growing collections of insects—especially beetles, which fascinated him all his life. He may well have continued this life of indolence forever had it not been for a Cambridge professor and friend, Reverend John Henslow, who recommended Charles for an unpaid position on a ship that had been commissioned to chart the coastline of South America and catalog information about the climate, inhabitants, wildlife, and plants they observed along the way.

The letter officially inviting him to join the expedition of the HMS *Beagle* arrived in August 1831. He would serve as "gentleman's companion" to the ship's master, Captain Robert FitzRoy.[5] Although Darwin wrote later that he served as the ship's naturalist, that was not entirely true, since the ship's doctor officially held that title. However, his interest in nature and collecting would prove to be a valuable asset in due time.

The voyage turned out to be a long one—five years at sea before all was said and done—and without pay. In fact, Charles would have to pay five hundred pounds for the privilege. At first, he was surprised and disappointed by Henslow's recommendation. He had no stomach for sailing and became seasick whenever he came near a boat. But, as he wrote later in his diary, his father was angry and disappointed that he had shown so little interest in a career, and Charles understood that his life of idleness could not continue indefinitely.

"To my deep mortification," he wrote in his journal, "my father once said to me, 'You care for nothing but shooting, dogs, and rat-catching, and you will be a disgrace to yourself and all your family.'"[6]

After thinking it over, Charles realized that the journey aboard the *Beagle* might turn out to be a spectacular adventure after all, with opportunities for visiting new and exotic places. He would have plenty of time for hunting, exploring, collecting, and keeping a journal of his experiences, which he might be able to turn into a book of some sort upon their return.

Exactly what Charles would be doing on the ship wasn't entirely clear. He had no nautical experience or skills. However, as Reverend Henslow informed him, the ship's captain was a gentleman of some importance—great grandson of King Charles II and heir of a great fortune—while the rest of the crew were mostly common sailors. Having a gentleman like Charles Darwin on board as a companion would provide suitable dinner conversation, someone with whom the captain could discuss such things as literature and the theater during their long and challenging voyage.

By the time they set sail, on December 27, 1831, Charles was genuinely excited to be taking part in such a dramatic adventure. He even boasted to his old Cambridge friends at the Glutton Club, "The scheme is a most magnificent one. We spend about 2 years in S. America, the rest of time larking round the world."[7]

He predicted he would beat them all in telling lies about his adventures when he returned.

### THE SEEDING OF THE THEORY

The common understanding of Charles Darwin, which has been taught in public schools and universities around the world for more than half a century, is that the idea of "evolution by natural selection" dawned on the great man suddenly and without warning when he first encountered the oddly shaped tortoises and finches of the Galapagos Islands. This version of the story has been repeated incessantly, as if the HMS *Beagle* set sail to the Pacific specifically to find such evidence, and that Charles' understanding of what he had discovered hit him in a blinding flash of inspiration. But this is far from the truth. In fact the basic premises of the theory did not even originate with Darwin.

Long before the *Beagle* set sail, Charles had already read Charles Lyell's influential book *Principles of Geology*, which challenged traditional beliefs about geological time and the formation of the earth. The book had been a gift from another Cambridge friend and mentor, the geologist Adam Sedgwick, who would later become famous for his work on the geological formations of the Cambrian Era. Lyell's book was strongly opposed to the biblical concept of creation and insisted that the earth was much older than commonly believed.

During his studies at Edinburgh, Charles had read the work of the French naturalist Jean Baptiste Lamarck, who was among the first to use the term *evolution* in reference to the adaptation of plants and animals over long periods of time due to changes in their environment. In his first important book, *Zoological Philosophy*, Lamarck stated that changes in plants or animals could be transmitted by natural heredity to the next generation. Thus transmutation could occur between species in a slow and predictable manner, so that over time an ape, such as the orangutan, could evolve into a man.

Of course, Charles had also read the writings of his grandfather, Erasmus Darwin. He read each of the new editions of *Zoönomia* as they were published. The book was highly successful and remained in print for many years. Clearly Charles was not the first—nor even the first Darwin—to propose a radical theory of a nontheistic origin of the species.

In fact, there is no reason to believe that when Charles embarked on the *Beagle* he had any idea of developing an alternate theory of origins. But circumstances brought about by his experiences on the voyage would later give him the platform for launching such a theory. His friend Reverend Henslow had suggested that Charles collect specimens of the native flora and fauna of South America and surrounding islands whenever the ship's crew made landfall. He knew this was just the sort of thing Charles would enjoy, not only because it allowed him to pursue his hobby of collecting, but also because he would be able to help supply food for captain and crew by shooting wild game during their forays on shore.

The voyage itself was agonizing for Charles. He was constantly seasick and was forced to seek refuge in his hammock for days and even weeks at a time. He couldn't wait to go ashore and explore the fascinating, but very dangerous, tropical terrain along the coast. At each port of call they made new discoveries—in places such as Patagonia, the Falkland Islands, and, most famous, the Galapagos Archipelago.

It was the first time any of the ship's crew had ever encountered creatures such as armadillos, ostriches, kinkajous, capybaras, agoutis, or llamas. They shot and ate them all and packed the bones off to England in large wooden crates. Thanks to an informal course in taxidermy he had taken during his student days in Edinburgh, Charles was able to stuff and mount a number of specimens and to provide rough pencil sketches of the birds and animals he encountered, along with their habitats.

Eventually, Charles crated and shipped hundreds of specimens—not only animals, birds, and insects but fossils and minerals of every sort—back to Cambridge. Henslow and his colleagues, many of whom were accomplished naturalists, busily cataloged and registered the previously unknown specimens and placed the most important ones on public display. By the end of the five-year voyage of the *Beagle*, there were warehouses and museums brimming with the artifacts Charles had collected.

Other experiences that later influenced Charles' evolutionary thinking were his trips ashore in Chile, Peru, Argentina, and Tierra del Fuego at the tip end of South America. These excursions provided eye-opening encounters with the native inhabitants. Taking off across the Pampas on horseback at one point, Charles traveled for several days with the gauchos and ran into indigenous tribes. By the time he rejoined the crew of the *Beagle*, his journals suggest, he had formed strong opinions about the inferiority of the primitive peoples he encountered there, and these added yet another complex layer to his notions about species development and the "favoured races."

## THE ACCIDENTAL SCIENTIST

Arriving in Plymouth, England, on October 2, 1836, Charles was shocked to discover that he was already a well-known man. Like everyone else in his family, he assumed he would be taking up his new post as a country parson. But, in fact, Henslow and Sedgwick had made him famous through the papers they had written and the lectures they had given about the various oddities they examined in his unique collection of specimens. They had even registered one rare species in Darwin's name. Charles was delighted, and settled into the role of scientist and naturalist with ease. At long last he had found a calling.

*The notion that Charles Darwin returned from his adventures on the Galapagos Islands with a full-fledged theory of evolution is simply false.*

On the other hand, Captain FitzRoy, who had provided him the chance to travel and explore and to make endless shipments of stones and bones back to England, became increasingly resentful of Charles' success. The charting operations and meteorological reports he had painstakingly prepared were ignored. His name was hardly mentioned in conversations regarding the voyage of the *Beagle*, and he was especially disturbed that Charles was proposing a radical and apparently atheistic interpretation of his findings. As a result, FitzRoy turned his back on Darwin and returned to his naval career, eventually serving as governor of New Zealand. Some have suggested that his suicide three decades later was due in part to the guilt he felt for being an accessory to Darwin's fame and fortune.

### WEAVING THE EVOLUTIONARY WEB

The notion that Charles Darwin returned from the voyage and his adventures on the Galapagos Islands with a full-fledged theory of evolution is simply false. His mind was full of the ideas he had gleaned from the writings of Lyell, Lamarck, and his grandfather, Erasmus Darwin—all of which was brewing in his head and taking shape slowly in his notebooks. But his own ideas were slow in coming.

He continued to write and speak about his discoveries without focusing too closely on the biological leaps that would ultimately become known as Darwin's Theory of Evolution. He published his own journal of the expedition and collaborated with FitzRoy in the official report of their achievements, but he was still insecure about how to interpret his discoveries regarding the apparent adaptation and transformation of species he had observed.

He developed a long-distance correspondence with American botanist and Harvard professor Asa Gray, who helped Charles to flesh out his own thinking on the distribution of variations within plant and animal species. But by the time he settled into a serious review of his notebooks from the *Beagle* expedition, he hadn't yet made any connections between the various tortoise shells or finches' beaks that played such a large role in his theory. He wasn't even certain which islands those specimens had come from. It was only after a theory began to take shape in his mind—with input from Gray, Lyell, Sedgwick, Robert Grant, and others—that he put the pieces together.

Charles continued to work at a steady pace for more than eight years, slowly assembling the pieces of a very complex puzzle. By 1844 he had completed drafts of several chapters of *The Origin of Species,* but was reluctant to finalize any of it since none of his friends and colleagues agreed with his assumptions about species transmutation and the possibility of blind evolution. Complicating matters even further was the fact that his wife was still a nominal Christian who found the atheism at the root of his theories disturbing.

This pattern of advance and retreat might have continued indefinitely if he had not come across a small book by an anonymous author called *Vestiges of the Natural History of Creation.* Even though the book was the work of a nonscientist, and superficial in many ways, it was bolder and grander in some respects than anything Darwin was proposing. The author—revealed forty years later to be a Scottish journalist named Robert Chambers—had laid out a startling image of creation, tracing the origins of life from the outer limits of space to the most common living organisms. As one biographer put it:

> Everything was there: astronomy, geology, botany, biology, paleontology. *Vestiges of Creation* was an international sensation, going through edition after edition. Darwin had been scooped. How could this anonymous author have so thoroughly guessed at Darwin's theory?[8]

In fact, complex theories of nontheistic evolution had been around at least since the first century BC, when the Roman philosopher and poet Lucretius wrote *De Rerum Natura (On the Nature of Things)*, proposing that all life sprang from a single source. Five hundred years earlier, the Greek philosopher Anaximander had suggested much the same thing. But the success of *Vestiges* came as a shock to Charles and forced him to speed up his efforts to bring his thoughts and ideas together. This was, after all, his big idea, and he wasn't sharing it with anyone.

As he neared completion of his magnum opus, Darwin was greeted by one more surprise. A scientific paper arrived in the mail from the English naturalist Alfred Russel Wallace, laying out a new theory of evolution. As he read it, Darwin realized that Wallace's theory was dangerously close to his own. He was tempted to bury it, ignore it, or perhaps discredit the author in some way. But his sense of honor would not allow him to do that. Instead he discussed it with a group of friends, who arranged for papers by both Darwin and Wallace to be read at a meeting of the Linnean Society in London.

The reading took place in November 1858. By the time the papers were read aloud by the secretary of the society, near the end of a long evening, many in the audience were already nodding off, and few of them perceived the potential impact of what they were hearing.

### The Darwinian Facts of Life

On November 24, 1859, a year after that first public presentation of his theory, an abstract of Darwin's book was published in London with the ponderous title *On the Origin of Species by Means of Natural Selection, or the Preservation of Favoured Races in the Struggle for Life.* In it, Darwin described how advanced species evolve from more primitive ones by means of natural selection over an immense span of time.

In a simplified restatement of Darwin's principal claims, the American biologist Ernst Mayr referred to Darwinian evolution as a composite theory made up of five categories. These include:

1. *Evolution as Such.* This expresses Darwin's view that the world is not constant or recently created, nor perpetually cycling, but is steadily changing, and that all living organisms are transformed in time.

2. *Common Descent.* This is the theory that every group of organisms descended from a common ancestor, and all groups of organisms—including animals, plants, and microorganisms—may be traced back to a single origin of life on earth.

3. *Multiplication of Species.* This theory explains the origin and radiation of organic diversity. It suggests that species multiply, either by splitting into daughter species or by *budding*, which is by the establishment of geographically isolated founder populations that evolve into new species.

4. *Gradualism.* According to this theory, evolutionary change takes place through the gradual change of populations and not by the sudden production of new individuals that represent a new type.

5. *Natural Selection.* According to this part of Darwin's theory, evolutionary change comes about through the abundant production of genetic variation in every generation. The relatively few individuals who survive, owing to a particularly well-adapted combination of heritable characteristics, give rise to the next generation.[9]

Of Darwin's several fundamental assumptions, the two best known are the interrelated concepts of "survival of the fittest" and "natural selection." Survival of the fittest is the theory that when vital resources such as food and shelter are limited by environmental conditions, survival rates naturally decline and only the fittest survive, thus keeping species populations in balance. Natural selection refers to the concept that individuals less suited to the environment are less able to compete for food, shelter, and breeding partners, while individuals that are better adapted are more likely to survive, and more likely to reproduce and leave their heritable traits to future generations. These principles were the core of Darwin's hypothesis.

## THE FIRST SHOTS OF THE BATTLE

While the reaction of Darwin's peers following the Linnean presentations was muted, public reaction to *The Origin of Species* was immediate and often hostile. The book was perceived not only as wild and unsubstantiated speculation but a frontal assault on Judeo-Christian theology. Darwin's suggestion that humans had evolved from lower forms such as apes was vigorously attacked and caricatured in periodicals such as *Punch, Vanity Fair,* and *Harper's.* On several occasions newspapers and magazines printed cartoons of Darwin, with his face superimposed on the body of a monkey.

Over the last 150 years, Darwin's theories have been praised and cursed with equal passion, and the debate continues to this day. Although Darwin spent a great deal of time and space discussing the basic principles of his theory, he spent very little time defending them. Instead he spent most of his time at his home in Kent while free thinkers such as the biologist Thomas Henry Huxley—who became known as Darwin's Bulldog—took on all challengers, enthusiastically fanning the evolutionary flame until it took hold and began to spread exponentially.

*Thomas Huxley—who coined the term* agnostic—*saw Darwinism as the perfect refutation of the religious beliefs he had long since rejected.*

When asked later why he had so vigorously defended Darwin's ideas, Huxley said he did so not because of Darwin's scientific speculations, which seemed fanciful, but because of the theological and moral implications of the theory.[10] Huxley—who coined the term *agnostic* to describe those who believe there is not enough evidence to confirm or deny the existence of God—saw Darwinism as the perfect refutation of the religious beliefs he had long since rejected.[11]

Darwin recognized at the time that the scarcity of evidence of transformation in the geological record could prove to be a serious obstacle to his theory. The fossil record does not provide "missing links." To date there have been no discoveries of transitional forms clearly linking one species to another. Instead, species appear suddenly in the fossil record, not gradually over time. But rather than conceding that his theory was flawed, Darwin insisted that the fossil record was imperfect. The evidence for transformation, he said, had been destroyed by violent changes in the earth. He was convinced that, in time, geologists would uncover the evidence that would at last confirm his theory.

## DARWIN'S DELIBERATE EXCLUSION OF GOD

Darwin continued to write and pursue private research for the rest of his life, focusing on ants, earthworms, vegetable mold, and other organisms he hoped might provide evidence of transmutation. He never found it. Along the way he modified some of his early assumptions but never renounced any of his ideas. His second book, *The Descent of Man*, took his arguments regarding the nature of human evolution a step further, making it clear that he was speaking of a universe that had evolved over a great span of time. All forms of life evolved from the simplest of cells, he said, and humankind sprang from the loins of primates—a view that made no place for the Judeo-Christian God.

In assessing the impact of Darwinism over the past 150 years, some authors have suggested that Darwin never meant to deny the importance of religion or the agency of God as Creator. But this is not true. In a letter to Charles Lyell, written a month before publication of his book, Darwin said, "I would give absolutely nothing for the theory of natural selection, if it requires miraculous additions at any one stage of descent."[12]

Despite his protests, Charles Darwin was persuaded to add a statement to the conclusion of *The Origin of Species* allowing for the possibility that life had been "originally breathed by the Creator." This was something he deeply regretted, and four years later, after agonizing over his compromise, he wrote to J. D. Hooker, "I have long regretted that I truckled to public opinion, and used the [biblical] term of creation, by which I really meant 'appeared' by some wholly unknown process."[13]

Wallace had wanted Darwin to acknowledge religion and call for a "reconciliation between Science and Theology," but that would have been a bridge too far. As Benjamin Wiker observed, "Darwin's triumph has been to set ideological atheism as the default position of science; as the prism through which scientists are supposed to see the world and conduct their work."[14] If all of life is governed by "time and chance," as Darwin insisted, no other alternative was permissible.

This is certainly the position from which contemporary evolutionists such as the late Stephen Jay Gould, Richard Dawkins, and Daniel C. Dennett have approached their subject. But, again, *The Origin of Species* did not disprove the existence of God. Darwin merely assumed that God had no hand in the matter. He believed that everything had come from nothing, and this assumption was the audacious leap of faith that led him to devise an outlandish theory to prove it.

The underlying premise of Darwinism is materialistic, reductionist, and deliberately atheistic, the consequence of which was the elimination of any basis for morality in his hypothesis. If the purpose of evolution is merely survival of the fittest, then virtues such as compassion, humility, and tolerance are meaningless and self-defeating. In such a world, might always makes right and victory belongs to the strong. But Charles Darwin the country gentleman could never have lived by the logic of his own theories.

## A FACADE OF BELIEF

Even though Charles had rejected the tenets of the theology he once studied, he kept up his family ties to the church. The Darwin and Wedgwood families had long tempered their Anglican beliefs with a strong dose of Unitarianism, a form of Christianity that denied the doctrine of the Trinity and the existence of hell. Yet each of his ten children was baptized in the Church of England. They took communion there, as well, although Charles' wife, Emma, made the children turn their faces to the wall whenever the congregation recited the Trinitarian creed—"in the name of the Father, the Son, and the Holy Ghost."

Despite his own loss of faith, Charles remained an active supporter, assisted with local charities, and maintained the appearance of a Christian gentleman. When he died in 1882 at Down House, his home for more than forty years, Charles Darwin was buried at Westminster Abbey in London, among such towering figures as Gregory Chaucer, William Shakespeare, Henry VIII, and most of the kings and queens of England. Thomas Huxley was among those who made the arrangements. And despite the very real damage he had done to the faith, Darwin was given a Christian burial.

Since that time Darwin has been praised as one of the greatest figures in the history of science. But what is the real legacy of his radical ideas? What good or ill has come from the theory this country gentleman formulated and publicized to such resounding acclaim? Perhaps it is time for a critical reappraisal. In the following chapters we will examine these questions in greater detail.

# 3 EVOLUTION AND THE DECLINE OF CULTURE

*One Rabbi who was imprisoned at Auschwitz said that it was as though all the Ten Commandments had been reversed: thou shalt kill, thou shalt lie, thou shalt steal. Mankind has never seen such a hell. And yet, in a real sense, if naturalism is true, our world is Auschwitz. There is no good and evil, no right and wrong. Objective moral values do not exist.*

Dr. William Lane Craig, theologian and philosopher[1]

Those who watched the documentary series *Cosmos* are not likely to forget the introduction to each episode. The charismatic astronomer, the late Carl Sagan, stepped in front of the camera and in his resonant baritone voice intoned the weighty phrase, "The Cosmos is all there is or ever was or ever will be." While most viewers found Dr. Sagan and his program fascinating and appealing, most rational thinkers found his opening phrase and the conclusions he drew from it appalling. And with reason.

73

First of all, Sagan was arrogantly asserting something he could not possibly know. A fish confined to its pond might deny the existence of a rumored world of prairies and mountains. But as we who live in such a world know, the fish would be dead wrong. And confined as it was to its limiting pond, it would have no means of verifying the truth of its assertion. Since science is by definition limited to probing nature, scientists speak irrationally and without means of verification when they assert there is nothing beyond the limits of their instruments.

The second reason Sagan's statement is so appalling is because he was articulating a philosophy that has done untold damage to the stability of Western culture. This may at first seem an extreme statement; after all, how can a mere intellectual idea undermine an entire culture? It's because ideas have consequences. Our deepest beliefs are not mere intellectual concepts; they are the spring from which our actions flow.[2]

In this chapter we will see how this works. Since Darwinism began to infiltrate our most influential institutions, the results have been destructive. We will explore how pushing God out of the picture as the Author of moral values leaves a vacuum that is inevitably filled by the desire for personal gratification, destroying the cohesion of society by pulling people apart into autonomous units of self-centeredness. We will explore how the influence of Darwinism, supplemented by other unsettling theories, has corrupted the arts by removing objective standards for meaning, and how it has caused entertainment to degenerate into license and perversion. As this chapter shows, ideas do indeed have consequences. Many scientists understand this, and yet they remain doggedly committed to promoting their destructive theory because they believe it gives them freedom from moral restraint.

## The Empty Philosophy of Naturalism

Darwinian evolution is, by definition, a naturalistic and materialistic view of the origins of life. The philosophy of naturalism is the belief that everything in our common experience can be explained by the laws of nature without reference to any sort of moral, spiritual, or supernatural force. Naturalistic philosophy makes no place for God, the moral law, or absolute right and wrong. As Carl Sagan asserted, nature is all there is.

The naturalistic view of the cosmos eliminates the concept of the supernatural. It excludes belief in God not only as Creator but also as the source of moral and ethical values. Whatever moral values we commonly subscribe to in society, the naturalistic philosophers tell us, are merely practices that simplify our lives by reducing conflict. If we believe that keeping to the right on a busy sidewalk helps us avoid chaos, that's the moral choice. Or if we believe that removing individuals with severe disabilities from society will help to limit reproduction and keep the breeding stock pure, that, too—as was originally believed by doctrinaire Darwinists—would be, in their view, a moral choice.[3]

As a Darwinist, we will naturally believe that the ethical or moral restraints we endure are arbitrary, and the social values we live by are merely a practical response to the demands of the environment. As a relatively insignificant part of nature, humans discover how to survive in their environment by trial and error. There is no moral law, no inherent truth except the truth we discover in the laws of nature, and no ultimate meaning beyond our temporary physical existence.

Contemporary sociobiologists Michael Ruse and Edward O. Wilson have written that morality is merely an adaptation of our species to further our reproductive ends. "In an important sense," they wrote, "ethics as we understand it is an illusion fobbed off on us by our genes to get us to cooperate."[4] Once again we see the specter of "illusion" so easily invoked by the evolutionists. Ethics and morals are only convenient illusions with no binding authority.

Here also, the philosophy is very much in accord with Darwin's own views. Ethical and moral choices, he said, are the natural expression of sympathy. Much like the virtues of love and courage, they are by-products of nature. He believed that vices (bad behaviors) are simply a consequence of the struggle for survival. Behaviors that offend community standards may be uncomfortable for some, and may be shunned by others, but in themselves they are not immoral—

merely inconvenient. A mother's instinct to protect her child is natural, but so is infanticide. Caring for family members is natural, but so is euthanasia, even if the deceased happens to be our next of kin.[5] This is the voice of naturalism speaking.

Believers understand that God provides a solid basis for morality, which itself provides the standards of right and wrong for all men and women throughout all time. This standard is absolute and universal. Its tenets are implanted in the human psyche and, with surprisingly little variation, have been adopted by all societies throughout recorded history. These principles of morality are obviously not natural. That is, we know they do not have their origins in the natural world because they often require men and women to act in ways that are not natural—ways that defy the instinct for self-preservation. There is nothing natural about a neighbor running into a fiery building to rescue a child or a soldier throwing himself on a grenade to save his buddies or telling the truth when a lie might save his life. Actions such as these do not preserve one's own genes or insure that the fittest survive. Yet such acts occur all the time, and they have no natural explanation. They come from motives and beliefs that are beyond the merely natural.

## Materialism: Naturalism's Ugly Cousin

Materialism in science is the view that there is no substance other than matter. The interactions of natural forces involve both energy and mass, but they are entirely material processes. A materialist view of nature denies any sort of spiritual transcendence and affirms only the reality of the physical world. Everything we observe in our common experience—including thoughts, feelings, mind, and human emotions—can be explained in terms of physical processes, beyond which nothing exists.

The materialist worldview was the belief system of Karl Marx and Friedrich Engels, who formulated the theory of *dialectical materialism* that would become the cornerstone of twentieth-century Communism. According to Marx and Engels, social change is the result of constant struggle between opposites. Since all human actions are motivated by naturalistic and materialistic concerns, they said, societies naturally become corrupt due to the acquisition of power and property by the ruling class. Therefore, to restore balance, it is necessary to overthrow the ruling class periodically and return power to the people.

*The connection between Darwin's big idea and the killing fields of Soviet Russia, Eastern Europe, Red China, and Pol Pot's Cambodia is not accidental.*

Without lingering on the details, the legacy of that view has left an indelible mark on the soul of mankind, with the deaths of more than one hundred million men, women, and children, murdered, beaten, and starved to death to achieve the radical dreams of the Marxist philosophers. Of course, none of this was imagined by Charles Darwin. The country gentleman in him would have been horrified by the thought; but the connection between Darwin's big idea and the killing fields of Soviet Russia, Eastern Europe, Red China, and Pol Pot's Cambodia is not accidental. They are patches from the same philosophical quilt.

*The Origin of Species* was published in 1859, eleven years after Marx had expounded his philosophy of "scientific socialism" in *The Communist Manifesto.* Yet while Marx's ideas were being consumed mainly within a small circle of political activists, Darwin was the recipient of international acclaim. The theory of natural selection and random mutation was being debated across Europe and beyond, and Marx was profoundly jealous. Nevertheless, Marx sent a copy of the second edition of his major work, *Das Kapital,* to Darwin, which the country gentleman placed on the shelf unread—thanks in large part, many believe, to the sensibilities of his Christian wife.

For those who believe that morality is optional and ethical behavior is merely a social compromise, nothing is forbidden. Everything is permitted because there is no transcendent Creator to validate absolute standards of morality. But the unavoidable result of such thinking is social and moral chaos. Without firm cultural standards capable of restraining our darker impulses, it is impossible to maintain order in society. Citizens who reject moral absolutes are a threat to themselves and others. Their promises mean nothing. Their desires and private passions become a law unto themselves, until they are forcibly restrained by a more powerful authority. Indeed, in a Darwinian world, power becomes the controlling force of society. The strongest dictate the rules according to their own wants and whims and enforce them on the rest. In such a view, there is no purpose or meaning to anything man does beyond simple survival.

## The Banishing of Morality

Such extremes in application of the theory may be rare in our culture today, but the theory of evolution promotes just such a worldview. Clarence Darrow, famous for his role in the "Scopes Monkey Trial" of 1925, expressed the evolutionist's creed very well: "The purpose of man is like the purpose of a pollywog," he said, "to wiggle along as far as he can without dying, or to hang to life until death takes him."

Without purpose or a moral order, life is meaningless, and the choices one makes are ultimately empty and vain. This is the image captured by the writer of Ecclesiastes:

> I denied myself nothing my eyes desired;
> I refused my heart no pleasure.

My heart took delight in all my work,
and this was the reward for all my labor.
Yet, when I surveyed all that my hands had done
and what I had toiled to achieve,
everything was meaningless, a chasing after the wind;
nothing was gained under the sun.[6]

Emptiness without consolation; labor without reward. And what is the price of such folly to society? Benjamin Wiker offered this sobering assessment:

We live in a time of complete moral revolution, when moral boundaries are being crossed so quickly that they fly past in a blur like so many telephone poles, as we hurtle into the new millennium. If we flipped through newspapers during the last half-century we would see the divorce rate blossom, the introduction and wild spread of legalized abortion, sexual hysteria, men marrying men, women marrying women, in vitro fertilization of a grandmother with the eggs of her daughter fertilized by her son-in-law, pedophiles clamoring for legal recognition, partial-birth infanticide, the marketing of "fresh" baby parts from abortion clinics, and now a British panel recommending human cloning for cell research. Interesting. Very interesting.[7]

Interesting, perhaps. But the carnage of such a moral breakdown is unspeakable. No one can question whether these changes in the social order have actually occurred; the only question in the minds of most thoughtful men and women today is whether or not the changes are for the better. Dr. Wiker, like most Christians today, is clearly disturbed by the loss of cultural standards. But how do the promoters of today's neo-Darwinian worldview react to these changes?

"Our willingness to accept scientific claims that are against common sense is the key to an understanding of the real struggle between science and the supernatural," wrote the evolutionary biologist Richard Lewontin. "We take the side of science in spite of the patent absurdity of some of its constructs, in spite of its failure to fulfill many of its extravagant promises of health and life, in spite of the tolerance of the scientific community for unsubstantiated just-so stories, because we have a prior commitment—a commitment to materialism."[8]

Lewontin, who has been hailed as a pioneer in the field of molecular evolution, makes no apology for his antirational stance. Rather, he says that, as an evolutionary biologist, he pays homage to a materialistic construct that adamantly rejects theological answers to life's questions. He wrote: "Materialism is an absolute, for *we cannot allow a Divine Foot in the door* (emphasis added)."[9]

In such astounding statements we see yet again the specter of illusion that haunts the materialistic worldview. Darwinists such as

Lewontin say, in effect, we realize special creation fits and explains the reality we see, and we realize our own explanation does not. Yet we choose to defy reason and reject the evidence, clinging to our illusions because it fits our naturalistic philosophy and frees us from any moral responsibility to a supernatural God.

Perhaps no one has done a better job of explaining the rationale behind the intellectual rejection of conventional morality than the grandson of Darwin's Bulldog, Thomas Huxley. Famous in his own right as a novelist and cultural critic, Aldous Huxley wrote in 1937 that the well-educated young men of his generation—not unlike the sixties generation in our own country—were at war with conventional morality for personal reasons. Christian morality was confining, but the idea of "meaninglessness" promised a sort of political and sexual liberation. He wrote:

> The liberation we desired was simultaneously liberation from a certain political and economic system and liberation from a certain system of morality. We objected to the morality because it interfered with our sexual freedom; we objected to the political and economic system because it was unjust. The supporters of these systems claimed that in some way they embodied the meaning (a Christian meaning, they insisted) of the world. There was one admirably simple method of confuting these people and at the same time justifying ourselves in our political and

erotical revolt: we could deny that the world had any meaning whatsoever.[10]

Huxley's rejection of morality wasn't the result of new scientific discoveries but merely the protest of a generation of overprivileged, effete young intellectuals against the mores of a sexual and political system they hated. This was precisely the sort of liberation Charles Darwin had offered them in *The Origin of Species*, demonstrating scientifically that human life, the universe, and everything else had come into being over an immense span of time without the input or agency of any supernatural being. No God, no Creator, no purpose, no moral absolutes. Just sheer dumb luck.

Sadly, however, the implications of this calculated and self-serving worldview are easy to see—they appear almost every day in the headlines. For at least the last half century, untold millions have been force-fed the materialistic assumptions of Darwinism and, as a result, many have lost the ability to understand the difference between right and wrong.

## The Deterioration of Culture

Fortunately, the perils of this way of thinking have not been lost on every member of the chattering classes. In his bestselling book on the effects of entropy as a social and cultural force, the American author and economist Jeremy Rifkin recognized thirty years ago the contradictions in the neo-Darwinian worldview and the chaos it creates. "We believe that evolution somehow magically creates greater overall value and order on earth," he said. "Now that the environment we live in is becoming so dissipated and disordered that it is apparent to the naked eye, we are beginning for the first time to have second thoughts about our views on evolution, progress, and the creation of things of material value."[11]

*For scientists and academics in their ivory towers, evolution has become the predominant view—more than a view, in fact. It is their theology.*

The writer's statements have been hotly debated in the media ever since, but there is no doubt he was speaking for many mainstream Americans who could see the world crumbling before their eyes. For scientists and academics in their ivory towers, evolution has become the predominant view—more than a view, in fact. It is their theology. But how have these materialistic and atheistic assumptions played out in the real world?

Rifkin said, "Evolution means the creation of larger and larger islands of order at the expense of ever greater seas of disorder in the world. There is not a single biologist or physicist who can deny this central truth. Yet, who is willing to stand up in a classroom or before a public forum and admit it?"[12]

Whether or not anyone was willing to admit it, the facts were undeniable. Former secretary of education William Bennett chronicled the chaos in the *Index of Leading Cultural Indicators* in the mid-1990s, illustrating the heartbreaking depths of America's decline. With the aid of detailed statistics, graphs, and charts, the index revealed a 500 percent increase in violent crime, an increase of more than 400 percent in births to unwed mothers, a doubling of the divorce rate, a 300 percent increase in the numbers of children living in single-parent homes, a 300 percent increase in teenage suicides, and a drop of more than seventy-five points in the average scores of high school seniors on the annual SAT exams.

That's the bad news. The really bad news is that the numbers have only gotten worse since that document was first published. While crime rates vary greatly across the country, and while the data will change from year to year—often disguised by politically motivated changes in reporting standards—it is still shocking to realize that America is now the most crime-ridden nation on the planet. This country leads the world in violent crime, abortions, and births to unwed mothers. Pornography, prostitution, pedophilia, and countless other previously forbidden activities are now practiced openly in virtually every city and town in America. As one observer has remarked, the average ten-year-old today knows more about sexually transmitted diseases than the average adult did twenty years ago. The divorce rate is now above 50 percent and steadily increasing.

We see a similar deterioration in art, music, and entertainment. Many contemporary painters have abandoned the classic guidelines of form, perspective, color harmony, and compositional balance in favor of deliberately nonobjective art such as the random paint drippings of Jackson Pollack and aimless lines and unidentifiable shapes of Richard Diebenkorn.

Even more meaningless are the postmodern constructs passed off as art in many modern museums. One example is the hanging of a completely blank canvas, which the artist explained by asserting that paint "violates the integrity of the canvas." Another artist displayed a young tree rooted in a pot of soil, claiming that a painting of a tree would have impaired the viewer's actual experience of a tree. A piano piece titled "4'33"" by composer John Cage consists of the pianist going to the piano and sitting at the keyboard for four minutes and thirty-three seconds without playing a note, then getting up and walking offstage.

Worse yet is the vulgarity and obscenity of popular music now available to every teenager with an iPod or an MP3 player, the rampant and graphic display of perversion and immorality on stage and screen, and the matter-of-fact acceptance of promiscuity and alternative lifestyles as normal in most TV programming.

# THE DEATH OF EVOLUTION

## MORAL AUTHORITY

These breakdowns in social stability, the growing acceptance of immorality, the willingness to kill the unborn and the "unfit," and the deterioration of art and entertainment are the natural consequences of the materialist worldview. As Dostoevsky said in *The Brothers Karamazov*, "If there is no immortality of the soul, there can be no virtue and therefore everything is permissible."[13] Evolution tells us exactly the same thing. Without the authoritative concept of a God who gives hope for a future beyond this life, where is the motivation to be moral? If man arose from a primeval swamp by sheer biological chance, then biological death will end his existence forever, so why not simply spend one's brief life grabbing for all the pleasure he can get with no concern about right or wrong? If there is no God to provide a rationale for morality, what difference does it make whether one observes society's rules or makes up his own to suit his whims?

When society begins to disdain overarching moral values, the sensual wants of the self become the driving force of life, and order and stability deteriorate. To paraphrase a former vice president, if there really is "no controlling moral authority," then what difference does it make if all these things are happening? To a few elites firmly committed to the materialist worldview, the disintegration of social norms does not matter. Why should it? Nothing matters in a mechanistic world with no meaning or purpose. There can be no reasonable doubt that the infusion of Darwinism into the major institutions of society has given many people a rationale for discarding traditional moral values and making the gratification of desire their primary motivation in life—and we see the evidence of that worldview everywhere today.

Fortunately, most Americans have enough common sense to realize that there is a moral crisis in our nation. While we can attribute much of it to the influence of the naturalism and materialism endorsed by Darwinian evolution, other influences have also played a part, including the explosion of new theories coming from the world of science.

Over the last century and a half, the world has undergone what sociologists have referred to as four great adjustments. They are adjustments to our collective worldview and philosophy brought about by the ideas of Darwin, Marx, Freud, and Einstein. Darwinian evolution, as we have seen throughout these pages, undermined the faith of millions in the majesty and authority of a Creator God. At about the same time, Marx was undermining social and political institutions with his theories of scientific socialism.

In the midst of all the monumental changes taking place in Europe during the first three decades of the twentieth century—World War I, the Bolshevik Revolution, the rise of both Fascism and Nazism—the relatively new science of psychiatry suddenly emerged as a topic of conversation in America's living rooms, along with the writings of Sigmund Freud and his theories of the ego, the id, and the labyrinth of the unconscious mind. Here was a whole new world of hidden psychological motivations, challenging everything most people had believed about the way we think and behave.

But then, while the world was still wrestling with all these ideas, Albert Einstein came along with news of the Special Theory of Relativity and later the General Theory of Relativity, proving that time, space, and energy are vastly different than anything scientists had previously imagined. Altogether, these four great adjustments were devastating to the common understanding of our world. And it would be decades before men and women of faith could offer a proper response.

## The Decline of Faith

It was no accident that faith in God would decline in Europe and America as these new ideas worked their way through the social fabric. While it is true that Albert Einstein had a vague notion of a benign creative force in the universe—best expressed in his famous quotation that "God does not play dice"—none of the four believed in a personal God, and the theories put forth by the other three were not only atheistic but aggressively antireligious.

It was also no accident that the groups most influenced by these factors would be the scientists and scholars who took up the challenge of disseminating the new ideas. In a recent study of leading scientists at twenty-one top-rated research universities in the United States, researchers found that 52 percent of the 1,646 individuals who participated have no religious affiliation. More than 31 percent said they do not believe in God, and another 31 percent said they don't know if there is a God. Just over 56 percent said they had not attended religious services during the preceding year, while just 9.7 percent said they have "no doubts about God's existence."[14]

These results were in striking contrast to another study, conducted in 2008 for the American Religious Identification Survey (ARIS), which reported that just 15 percent of American adults say they have no religious affiliation. Among those aged eighteen to twenty-nine the figure was higher, at 22 percent. But of the 54,461 adults who participated, 76 percent identified themselves as Christians. Although a decrease of 10 percent from a similar survey in 1990, the numbers were still much higher than those for scientists and scholars.[15]

The most interesting finding of the ARIS survey was the fact that, when speaking of personal beliefs rather than religious affiliation, 70 percent of the adults surveyed said they do believe in a personal God, while just 12 percent claimed to be atheists or agnostics, and 12 percent said they were deists—believing in a higher power but not necessarily a personal God. This means that a plurality of 82 percent continue to believe that—despite the claims of the atheists—God is alive and well in America.[16]

As a final note in this vein, atheists have insisted for years that religious people are just superstitious and will believe anything. To test that idea, the Institute for Studies of Religion at Baylor University commissioned a survey by the Gallup Organization to determine whether individuals who regularly attend religious services really are more likely to be superstitious than those who do not. Researchers first asked whether or not individuals in the survey had any religious affiliation, then they posed a series of questions, such as: Do dreams foretell the future? Did ancient advanced civilizations such as Atlantis exist? Can places be haunted? Is it possible to communicate with the dead?

When the results were tabulated, researchers found that just 8 percent of evangelicals and members of traditionally conservative denominations answered in the affirmative that, yes, those things are possible. However, nearly four times as many nonreligious respondents (31 percent) said that all those things were possible. This wasn't the answer the skeptics had expected.

Most of us have heard the expression, "When people stop believing in God, they don't believe in nothing. They believe in anything." Apparently the maxim is true. But the real miracle may be that so many professing Christians have been able to hold on to their faith and make sound moral choices based on their religious convictions while at the same time resisting the attempts of atheists, secular scientists, and educators to remove God from the conversation.

## A Faith with Ultimate Meaning

Holding on to one's faith in the face of ridicule and persecution is never an easy task, and it only gets harder as the push for atheism in academia and the media increases. But as we have shown in this chapter, the payoff to belief in God as Creator is enormous. Not only do Christians have the obvious hope of eternal life; they also find that belief in God gives them a stable, sane, and satisfying way of understanding the world. It gives them meaning as beings fashioned in the image of the Creator of the universe. It gives them purpose as his agents in the world. It gives them stability with overarching moral principles to guide them to a life of positive interaction with family and community. And, best of all, faith in the Creator God gives meaning to the emotion of love and our sense of awe when we behold the beauty and wonder of the cosmos. No materialistic philosophy comes close to offering any of that.

Belief in a Creator God fits the reality of life as we know it perfectly, whereas Darwinian evolution must continually claim that the reality we think we perceive is merely an illusion. These are only a few of the reasons that faith survives against all the odds. And the world of secular science is better off because of it—as we shall see in the following chapter.

# 4 MAKING SENSE OF FAITH AND SCIENCE

*The irony is devastating. The main purpose of Darwinism was to drive every last trace of an incredible God from biology. But the theory replaces God with an even more incredible deity: omnipotent chance.*

Dr. Theodore Roszak, professor emeritus of history,
California State University[1]

The final decades of the eighteenth century saw two major political revolutions on two continents: the American Revolution against England in 1776 and the French Revolution against the monarchy in 1789. While both revolutions were successful in throwing off tyranny, the resulting new governments of each country were founded on vastly different principles. The framers of the new American government recognized that law, power, rights, and freedoms were not determined by man but by God, and they took care to build that principle into our Constitution. As a result, they founded a nation of freedom and stability that grew in prosperity and influence like no other in the history of the world.

The French, on the other hand, were influenced by the rationalism of Enlightenment philosophers who believed that, by the power of reason alone, man could determine his own destiny. As a result, with no overarching, solidifying principles, the French Revolution degenerated into a bloody reign of terror and anarchy that left the nation in chaos for more than half a century.

The main difference in the two outcomes was that one placed God at the center and the other did not. In essence, this meant that one government was based on reality and the other on a man-made fantasy. For a century and a half, America in general continued to look to God as the center of government, culture, and private life. In the second half of the twentieth century, however, that outlook began to erode, and the results are becoming increasingly visible in the deterioration of morality, loss of freedoms, soaring crime rate, and alarming weakening of the family. Placing God at the center of any endeavor is the key to stability, order, and meaning. Removal of God always leads to bad results.

As we will see in this chapter, the same principle holds true in the world of science. With God at the center of scientific inquiry, the sciences flourished. The men who first developed the scientific method made great strides because they believed the physical world was rational and orderly because it was created by a rational and orderly Creator. This view was so strong that when Darwinian evolution first entered the picture, most people saw it as an attempt to replace the solid foundations of scientific thought with a theory built on thin air. The theory didn't accord with observable reality. Its weaknesses were immediately apparent and were challenged as fanciful illusions. The theory might have died a natural death if not for the fact that skeptics, free thinkers, and agnostics were quick to see the potential of Darwin's ideas to transform the foundations of culture. As they tweaked it with adjustments and newly contrived explanations, they managed to entrench an unproven theory as official dogma in our most influential institutions.

The good news is that while the Darwinists often appear to be winning the battle of ideas, they have failed to convince the American people that the theory of evolution is reasonable or true. While scientific naturalism and evolutionary biology remain strong in certain institutions—including universities, public schools, and the mainstream media—they lack authority among the public at large, as surveys cited in these pages will show. Darwinism, quite simply, does not fit with reality because it denies the possibility of an intelligent Creator and ascribes to blind chance the creative powers that belong to God alone. That, in a nutshell, is the story to be examined in this chapter.

## THE FAITH-BASED ROOTS OF THE SCIENTIFIC METHOD

It is generally understood that modern science first emerged in Europe during the sixteenth and seventeenth centuries. Although there were advances in technology, mathematics, and philosophy in China, India, and the Arabian peninsula prior to the Middle Ages, the kind of careful investigative inquiry and experimentation we recognize today as the scientific method was a uniquely Western phenomenon. The expansion of trade between AD 500 and 1500 opened up the West to new ideas from far and wide, but the essential tools of thought and experimentation that made science possible were, above all, gifts of the Christian faith.

For nearly two thousand years, the most widely accepted explanation for the origins and diversity of life in the natural world was the biblical account of *special creation*. Greek and Roman philosophers spoke of a great First Cause—the Prime Mover that set the cosmos in motion. This view, which was a major component of Aristotle's *Metaphysics*, was generally compatible with the biblical narrative and was assimilated into what became known as the *cosmological argument*. From the Middle Ages through the mid-nineteenth century, this was the dominant view. The biblical view of creation holds that all creatures great and small were created by God, each uniquely suited to its place in the natural order.

Contrary to popular myth, science was not at war with this explanation of the cosmos or with religion at all during its formative stages. Rather, as historian and author Rodney Stark pointed out, "these achievements were the culmination of many centuries of systematic progress by medieval Scholastics, sustained by that uniquely twelfth-century invention, the university."[2] Science and religion were inseparable companions, sharing in the task of penetrating the secrets of nature through the processes of reason, analysis, and systematic observation. Intellectual pursuits of this kind were the native terrain of medieval churchmen.

From the time of Augustine onward, Christian scholars believed in the logic and order of nature because they believed in a Creator who fashioned an orderly world out of chaos: "The earth was without form, and void; and darkness was on the face of the deep."[3] The words of the Hebrew text made it clear that the heavens were formless and void until God spoke forth and called the world into being *ex nihilo*—from nothing—separating light from darkness and dry land from the dark waters of oblivion. Because God imposed order on chaos and established natural laws to maintain that order, scholars understood that the structures and dynamics of the material creation would be orderly and consistent, and therefore subject to rational investigation. Modern science would never have been born without these basic assumptions about the nature of reality.

Furthermore, Christian scholars understood that the world is real. According to Eastern thought as represented by both Hinduism and Buddhism, the world is an illusion. Such a world is not reliable or reasonable, and the efforts of men to probe and explore the secrets of nature are destined to failure. But Christian scholars pursued knowledge of the cosmos and the natural sciences, as Stark said, "because they *believed* it *could* be done, and *should* be done [emphasis in the original]."[4]

The English philosopher Alfred North Whitehead expressed just such a view at Harvard during his Lowell Lecture series, saying that science first emerged in Europe because of widespread "faith in the possibility of science." Far from being an enemy of scientific inquiry, as secular scientists are inclined to say, the church actively and enthusiastically promoted the pursuit of knowledge and employed academics, scholars, and teachers to do just that.

For the better part of four hundred years, science was seen as the handmaiden of theology. Medieval and renaissance scholars were open to new discoveries because they believed that all truth is God's truth, and that everything in the natural order was made and ordained by God for our good.

The new technologies that were developed through the practical sciences made life easier and reduced suffering for everyone. No one could fail to appreciate the benefits of laborsaving devices, improved sanitation, water wells fed by windmills that were made possible in turn by pulleys and gears, and so many other inventions. These things affirmed the value of science and were a tribute to the power of reason and invention, which were made possible in turn by a practical understanding of nature's laws.

The very existence of the laws of nature meant that there had to be a Lawgiver. Otherwise, how was it possible to understand the natural laws and make accurate calculations based upon them? The Christian pioneers of science believed they were able to understand and apply these laws in many useful ways because God the Creator had made them accessible and given mankind the capacity to penetrate nature's secrets. This was the matrix through which modern science developed.[5]

## Darwin's Most Critical Missing Link

Prior to the developments that became known as "the new learning," science had been based more on philosophy than empirical research and observation. In Greek mythology the Earth goddess, Gaia, created humans and animals from stones. Aristotle disagreed with this idea (known as *abiogenesis*) that life could have evolved from inert matter, but he believed nevertheless that certain animals could arise from other organisms, and possibly from the earth itself. Surprisingly, this view survived into the sixteenth and seventeenth centuries, but in due time such notions were abandoned.

Yet in spite of all the advances of science over the past five centuries, Darwin's premise that life generated from nonliving matter is closer to Greek mythology than to the findings of modern science—a fact that has been proved in the laboratory. Five years after publication of Darwin's magnum opus, the French chemist and microbiologist Louis Pasteur conducted a series of experiments to determine whether or not very simple organisms could reproduce spontaneously without coming into contact with preexisting life. His experiments were conclusive and easily reproducible and showed that life comes only from other life.

Pasteur summarized his findings in the Latin phrase *"Omne vivum ex ovo,"* meaning, "All life comes from the egg." Or in more common language, living beings come only from other living beings, which is the underlying principle of the Law of Biogenesis. No matter how far and wide scientists have looked for exceptions to this principle, they find that when humans reproduce, they give birth to little humans— not monkeys or polar bears or jellyfish. Monkeys produce monkeys, and even with slight variations in the shapes and color of their shells, Galapagos turtles still produce little turtles.

Darwin's suggestion that life arose from a bolt of lightning striking a "warm little pond," thereby mysteriously creating the amino acids that would become the building blocks of life, was tested in 1952 by two researchers at the University of Chicago. During the 1920s, the Russian biochemist Aleksandr Oparin and the British geneticist J. B. S. Haldane had published papers suggesting that certain chemicals present in primitive oceans may have combined to form the self-reproducing organic materials that, when catalyzed by sunlight or an electrical discharge in a hydrogen-rich atmosphere, could have transformed inert materials into the first living cells. Both scientists believed there would have been very little oxygen in earth's early atmosphere but that the seas would have been full of other materials.

Thirty years later, these ideas were tested by two American chemists. Dr. Stanley Miller and his graduate student, Harold Urey, constructed a model of a primitive environment in the laboratory, using a mixture of water vapor, ammonia, methane, and molecular hydrogen. When the water was heated, gases emitted from the mixture were passed through a small electrical corona in order to induce a chemical reaction within the liquid.

By the end of the first day the water had turned pink, then red, and a week later when the scientists analyzed the mixture, they found three amino acids (glycine, alpha-alanine, and beta-alanine). In their view, they had successfully confirmed the Oparin-Haldane hypothesis.

When news of the experiment became public, the mainstream media went wild with speculations. At long last there actually seemed to be evidence that Darwin got it right. For several years Miller and Urey were hailed as the equals of Francis Crick and James Watson, who successfully identified the double helix structure of DNA. *Time* magazine even called the compound Miller and Urey formulated "the Adam molecule." Although the *Time* reporters admitted that "Professor Urey and Student Miller" did not believe they had actually created life, they nevertheless wrote that, "This was the hoped-for payoff . . . the building blocks of which proteins are made." And, they added:

> What they have done is to prove that complex organic compounds found in living matter can be formed, by chemical reactions, out of the gases that were probably common in the earth's first atmosphere. If their apparatus had been as big as the ocean, and if it had worked for a million years instead of one week, it might have created something like the first living molecule.[6]

Unfortunately for Miller and Urey, the passage of time has not been so kind to their theory. Among the first to challenge the Miller-Urey experiments were biologists who, while continuing to support the basic principles of evolution, disputed that the chemical compounds the Chicago team had chosen were the right ones. In 1972, the Nobel laureate Ilya Prigogine wrote in *Physics Today:*

> The probability that at ordinary temperatures a macroscopic number of molecules is assembled to give rise to the highly ordered

structures and to the coordinated functions characterizing living organisms is vanishingly small. The idea of spontaneous genesis of life in its present form is therefore highly improbable.[7]

In a 1976 journal article, the biophysicist and evolutionary biologist Dean Kenyon took issue with the circular reasoning Miller and Urey had used, guessing at the oxygen levels of the earth's early atmosphere, guessing at the chemical properties of the "warm little pond," and guessing at the age of the earth when the process supposedly took place, and then saying that the earth had to be the way they described it based solely on the results their experiment produced. Kenyon wrote, "One cannot simply assume that it did take place and then argue that conditions on the prebiotic Earth must have been such as to allow it to occur." In other words, the desired results dictated the shape of the experiment.[8]

*"We have not the slightest chance of a chemical evolutionary origin for even the simplest of cells."*
—DR. DEAN H. KENYON, professor emeritus of biology, San Francisco State University

Years later, after reflecting at greater length on the arguments for the spontaneous appearance of simple life forms by mechanistic processes, Kenyon wrote, "We have not the slightest chance of a chemical evolutionary origin for even the simplest of cells."[9]

Eventually Dr. Kenyon would pay a price for his honest opinion, being removed from the classroom for expressing doubts about Darwinism, even though he was not alone in his view. Since that time dozens of highly credible specialists have added their voices to the controversy, agreeing that the odds against life forming in the way Miller and Urey suggested were prohibitively great. It became more and more apparent that Darwin's most essential link to credibility—a nontheistic explanation for the origin of life—was still missing.

### Evolution's Other Fatal Flaw—
### the Not-So-Simple Cell

By the end of the nineteenth century, faith in the theory of evolution was at a very low ebb and close to being rejected outright by the scientific community on both sides of the Atlantic. Forty years after publication of *The Origin of Species*, there were just too many problems with Darwin's narrative. The lack of transitional forms of any kind in the fossil record was seen as conclusive proof that the theory of evolution through random mutation and natural selection was unrealistic.

Yet in spite of widespread doubt and disappointment with the theory, biologists who saw the evolutionary hypothesis as a way of ridding the sciences of religious influence undertook a resuscitation of Darwin's ideas. The new approach, called *neo-Darwinism*, was essentially a synthesis of the theory of natural selection and the emerging science of population genetics. The new term was first introduced around 1890 with reference to studies by the German biologist August Weismann, whose experiments in cell biology actually disproved Darwin's claim that acquired characteristics could be passed from one generation to the next—which was essential for Darwin's view of natural selection. In his determination not to allow this damning new evidence to overturn Darwinism, Weismann turned to the theory of cellular alteration via genetic mutation to explain changes in species. But later research proved that even these modifications were insufficient to overcome the weaknesses in the evolutionary hypothesis.

In a recent interview with the scientist and engineer Walter L. Bradley, journalist and former atheist Lee Strobel pointed out that the simple one-cell organism at the beginning of the evolutionary chain turned out not to be such a simple organism after all. As the researchers have discovered, what Darwin had supposed to be a tiny blob of protoplasm—with the consistency of a speck of Jell-O—is in fact a high-tech factory, complete with its own artificial language and decoding systems.

Every cell in our bodies—and there are trillions of them—has a central memory bank that can store and retrieve massive amounts of information, very much like a high-speed computer. Precision control systems regulate transportation routes, shipping genetic components and operating instructions throughout the system. There are even proofreading and quality-control mechanisms within the cell that can detect and correct errors, and assembly lines that follow the principles of prefabrication and modular construction. There is also a replication system that allows the organism to duplicate itself at bewildering speeds. And all of this is happening simultaneously, in every living cell in our bodies.[10]

........................................................................................................

*The great discovery that Darwin and his defenders had missed was the complexity of the very organisms biologists assumed to be simple.*

........................................................................................................

The great discovery that Darwin and his defenders had missed throughout their long and tedious search for evidence of a materialistic origin of life was the complexity of the very organisms biologists assumed to be simple. Thanks to the discoveries of chemists and biologists using the latest state-of-the-art technology, we now know that there is nothing simple about the single cell. ID researchers like Michael Behe, William Dembski, Stephen Meyer, and Jonathan Wells have described the complex structure and function of biological machines that defy explanation by evolutionary principles.

Darwin's model proposed that natural selection is capable of picking and choosing the best features of any organism and, by gradual mutation over millions of years, transforming them into new and more highly adapted organisms. What researchers have actually found, however, is that microbiological systems throughout the biosphere exhibit a level of complexity that defies the gradualist approach. They understand that complex organs cannot come together piece by piece over millions of years.

William Paley, who was an opponent of evolutionary thinking in Darwin's time, understood that organic complexity defies evolution. He pointed specifically to the properties of the human eye, comparing it with a man-made telescope. Both the eye and the telescope are marvels of design; both employ the science of optics with great precision. Yet the eye is still more practical and adaptable. No telescope can match its sensitivity to sun and shade, its ability to change focus instantly, or its ability to accurately perceive three dimensions of space simultaneously.

Either the eye works from day one as an eye or it doesn't work at all. Half an eye, or some fraction of an eye, will not allow the creature to see or even survive. But now we know that it isn't only eyes, ears, the sensory organs, or the reproductive system that is irreducibly complex; every cell in our bodies, and in the bodies of every living organism, are engaged in operations at the microbiological level that are mind-bendingly complex. And the chances of any of these operations happening purely by chance—as the calculations of mathematicians like Roger Penrose (described in chapter three) reveal—are beyond even the most far-fetched limits of probability.

# THE DEATH OF EVOLUTION

Even Darwin recognized the problem with complex structures. In the final chapter of *The Origin of Species*, he wrote, "To suppose that the eye, with all its inimitable contrivances for adjusting the focus to different distances, for admitting different amounts of light, and for the correction of spherical and chromatic aberration, could have been formed by natural selection, seems, I freely confess, absurd in the highest possible degree."[11] But he was committed to his theory on personal and philosophical grounds, and nothing could dissuade him from it—not even common sense.

## RESISTING THE OBVIOUS CONCLUSION

The only logical conclusion in the face of such evidence, as Michael Behe said, is that evolution cannot answer the question of origins because it has determined, *a priori*, that there is no room for a First Cause or an Intelligent Designer in this picture. The folly of such a view should have been seen as far back as 1953 when Crick and Watson identified the structure of DNA not as a glob of tissue but as a highly complex information-passing polynucleotide chain. What these researchers found was essentially a high-tech computer network within the living cell, passing an incredible volume of complex information in chemical form throughout the entire biological system.

While the basic properties of DNA (deoxyribonucleic acid) and

RNA (ribonucleic acid) had been known for decades, Watson and Crick discovered that the DNA of most organisms is composed of two polynucleotide chains, twisted together in a coil in the shape of a double helix. The backbone of each polynucleotide chain consists of a sugar-phosphate sequence, and all along this chain information is being passed in intelligible coded patterns.

*"To suppose that the eye, with all its inimitable contrivances for adjusting the focus to different distances, for admitting different amounts of light, and for the correction of spherical and chromatic aberration, could have been formed by natural selection, seems, I freely confess, absurd in the highest possible degree."*

—Charles Darwin

Between 1990 and 2003, a team of scientists from the National Institutes of Health were able to identify and map all of the twenty to twenty-five thousand genes of the human genome, and to observe the actual information-passing dynamics of these biological structures. But, somehow, even this wasn't enough to convince the skeptics of the importance of the ID hypothesis.

## The Rise of the Intelligent Design Hypothesis

Although we have seen some of the basic principles of Intelligent Design throughout these pages, it will be helpful at this point to review the organization and objectives of the movement in a little more detail. According to leading proponents of the design movement (the Discovery Institute and the Center for Science and Culture), Intelligent Design refers to scientific research programs that are currently investigating structural questions about the origins of life on earth, along with the scientists, philosophers, and academics who are exploring evidence of design in nature.

The ID hypothesis holds that certain features of our world are best explained not by an undirected process but by an intelligent cause. This principle itself is not new. As far back as 1802, the paleontologist William Paley had introduced the principle in his book *Natural Theology: or, Evidences of the Existence and Attributes of the Deity, Collected from the Appearances of Nature*, with his famous metaphor of the Creator as Watchmaker. If you come across a stone in a meadow, he said, you don't spend much time wondering where it came from, since there are stones everywhere. However, if you find a pocket watch in the middle of a meadow, you may be surprised, since it is clearly a created object. Furthermore, if the watch keeps accurate time you will perceive that it was created by a very capable designer. Since we know that all the elements of our universe—the heavens, the earth, the animal kingdom, human society, and much else—are not only stunningly elegant but also logical, intricate, highly complex, and interrelated, we can know that the natural world is the handiwork of a supremely Intelligent Designer.[12]

ID researchers develop their data by observing objects that exhibit the types of information processing, as previously described, that can be readily identified as products of an intelligent cause. These techniques have been used to detect evidence of design in irreducibly complex biological structures, including the information content of DNA as well as the architecture of the universe. In particular, scientists involved in ID research have focused on the sudden appearance of biological diversity in the fossil record during the Cambrian explosion, which is estimated to have occurred as much as 530 million years ago.

Because of the false narrative that has seeped into the culture ever since the "Scopes Monkey Trial" of 1925, the term *creationism* is often used today as a derogatory term by secular scientists, educators, and the mainstream media, and the Genesis story of creation is derided as a fundamentalist myth. But Intelligent Design is not the same as creationism. Rather, the ID movement is an effort to detect empirically whether "apparent design" in nature is, in fact, the product of an intelligent cause.

The formal basis of creationism begins with the Genesis account. Creation scientists test the reliability of scientific theory based on how closely they support the theological narrative. Intelligent Design, on the other hand, begins with evidence from nature and attempts to assess what inferences can be logically drawn from those findings. Unlike creationism, the theory of

Intelligent Design does not attempt to identify the intelligent cause. While ID is compatible with a theistic view of creation, ID researchers make no effort to draw theological or metaphysical conclusions from their research.

## ANSWERS TO ID CRITICS

Some of the critics of Intelligent Design have recognized the differences between ID and creationism. For example, science historian Ronald Numbers is critical of the ID movement, but has said he agrees "the creationist label is inaccurate when it comes to the ID movement." The reason Darwinists have tried so hard to link ID to creationism, he says, is because they see this as "the easiest way to discredit Intelligent Design." If the secularists can show that Intelligent Design is only theology by another name, they may be able to prevent people from paying attention to it. In reality, however, the more they try to demonize the ID movement the more they reveal their fear of it.

"Intelligent design begins with the observation that intelligent agents produce complex and specified information." This is the position advocated by Discovery Institute scholars. If a natural object was designed, they say, it will contain high levels of information. To test whether or not complex information is present, researchers attempt to identify the level of complexity by reverse engineering the relevant biological structures. When they find evidence of irreducible complexity, they are able to conclude, naturally and logically, that these structures were, in fact, designed.

Another common claim is that supporters of ID want to force public schools to teach Intelligent Design, but this is not true. All major ID organizations oppose efforts to require the teaching of Intelligent Design by school districts or state boards of education. Attempts to mandate teaching of Intelligent Design only lead to more controversy and an environment that may be hostile to the principles of the theory.

Instead of mandating Intelligent Design, organizations such as the Discovery Institute and the Center for Science and Culture actually want to increase coverage of Darwinian evolution in textbooks. They believe it is important and scientifically responsible to teach both the strengths and weaknesses of Darwin's theory. Unfortunately, almost all public school districts in the U.S., Canada, Great Britain, and Western Europe teach only one side of the evolutionary hypothesis, which results in an incomplete and distorted understanding of the science involved and covers up its many unproved and nonscientific assumptions.

While ID supporters do not believe Intelligent Design should be a required subject in public schools, they believe there is nothing unconstitutional about discussing the scientific basis of Intelligent Design in the classroom. They also believe that scientists, university professors, researchers, and teachers who wish to discuss these ideas openly should not be penalized for their efforts. But apparently the rhetoric of tolerance and diversity that has been raised to cultlike status on many campuses over the last thirty years is a one-way street.

## THE INTOLERANCE OF DARWINISTS

The truth is, systematic discrimination against scientists, professors, researchers, and teachers who dare to question the Darwinian orthodoxy—or even attempt to discuss openly the principles of design and creation—is one of the most disturbing and underreported facts of our time. The actor Ben Stein began the 2008 documentary *Expelled* with a quick review of several cases in which individuals have been discriminated against for doubting the official doctrine of Darwinism. Thanks to the irrationality of Darwinist position and Stein's quirky sense of humor, he was able to make the perpetrators look silly; but this issue is not a laughing matter.

---

*Systematic discrimination against scientists, professors, researchers, and teachers who dare to question the Darwinian orthodoxy— or even attempt to discuss openly the principles of design and creation—is one of the most disturbing and underreported facts of our time.*

---

Students in university classrooms are routinely vilified by their professors for asking questions or merely expressing views that differ from the party line. In some cases, students have been kicked out of class, or out of college, for simply mentioning the problems with Darwinism or asking about alternative theories of origins. But the persecution and prosecution of schoolteachers, university professors, and professional researchers can go even further.

Dr. Dean Kenyon, mentioned earlier, was removed from his Biology 100 classroom at San Francisco State University in 1993 for expressing reservations about certain evolutionary positions and suggesting that the ID movement may have better answers in some areas. Kenyon, who holds a PhD in biophysics from Stanford University and completed postdoctoral studies at U.C. Berkeley, Oxford, and NASA, was humiliated by university administrators, not because he misled or misinformed his students, but because he broke the code of silence about the problems of Darwinism.

In a review of Ben Stein's documentary, Dr. Ray Bohlin, a molecular biologist and fellow of the Discovery Institute, recounted a number of cases where scientists were victims of the evolutionary thought police. In one, a professor with PhD degrees in biology and evolution, was locked out of his office and had all his research privileges denied for the sin of raising questions about Darwin's hypothesis. When he was terminated, a U.S. senator began asking questions and was told it was just a big mistake. Soon enough the facts of the case became painfully clear, but it didn't help the professor get his job back.[13]

In another incident, an accomplished biology instructor was demoted and fired for simply including evidence contrary to Darwinism along with evidence for it. On still another campus, a popular and widely published astronomer was denied tenure even though he had published over four times the necessary peer-reviewed articles. The problem was that he was known to be a supporter of Intelligent Design. Even though he had never mentioned that fact in any of his classes, he was denied advancement in his career. These are just a few of the most recent cases, and there are literally dozens more.

Actually, this type of discrimination has been going on for years. In his 1984 book addressing the problems of intellectual dishonesty, Dr. I. L. Cohen offered this eye-opening comment from a biologist at a major university:

> There are certainly a good number of scientists who now reject the concepts of evolution—not on religious grounds, but on strictly scientific grounds. Most of them are keeping their own counsel. Outwardly they support evolution (so as to be in step with their peers) but inwardly they have second thoughts on the subject. It is not too easy to take a stand against the beliefs of the majority, and expose oneself to ridicule, especially when one's

job and academic and professional prospects are on the line. It is only the very brave and those highly placed scientists whose standings are universally acknowledged (and thus, secure) that can afford to contradict the general trend.[14]

Dean Kenyon's case was just one of many, and the discrimination has only gotten worse since that 1993 incident. But there is ample evidence that highly regarded scientists with books and scientific papers to their credit have been targets of vicious slander and hate-mail campaigns. A list compiled by Dr. Jerry Bergman in his 2008 book *Slaughter of the Dissidents*, reveals the scope of these persecutions.[15]

Over the last fifteen hundred years, the scientific community has said that sound, objective, and reliable results can only be obtained when all relevant theories have been tested and all objections are resolved. But clearly this is not happening in the evolution debates. The secular science community has joined forces with the media, the education establishment, the universities, and even members of the general public to make sure that the weaknesses of Darwinism are never exposed.

To maintain their defensive position, they have built an impregnable wall around this sacred mount. But in the process they've raised more questions than they've answered. At this moment, millions of men and women are beginning to ask questions, probing the bulwarks of Darwin's redoubt, looking for honest answers. They're beginning to wonder whether science without faith makes sense. Sooner or later even Darwin's staunchest defenders will have to answer that one.

Meanwhile, we cannot help but be inspired by the integrity, honest inquiry, and courage of those in the ID movement. Many of them have laid their careers on the line and paid the price simply for daring to question the irrationality of Darwinism, and for proposing a rational, scientifically valid alternative. Their example should inspire each of us to seek the truth and hold to it whatever the cost. After all, it is the truth that makes us free.

# 5 RESTORING MEANING AND PURPOSE

*For the scientist who has lived by his faith in the power of reason, the story ends like a bad dream. He has scaled the mountain of ignorance; he is about to conquer the highest peak; as he pulls himself over the final rock, he is greeted by a band of theologians who have been sitting there for centuries.*

Dr. Robert Jastrow, physicist; founding director,
NASA's Goddard Institute for Space Studies[1]

One early victim of Darwinian evolution was the nineteenth-century scientist George John Romanes, who was a believer in creation until he became a disciple of Darwin and turned to atheism. Romanes, who was also a poet, expressed deep pain over what he lost when he abandoned his Christian faith: "With this virtual negation of God the universe to me has lost its soul of loveliness . . . when at times I think, as think at times I must, of the appalling contrast between the hallowed glory of that creed which once was mine, and the lonely mystery of existence as I now find it—at times I shall ever feel it impossible to avoid the sharpest pang of which my nature is susceptible."[2]

For Romanes, Darwinian atheism had taken all the beauty, meaning, purpose, and hope out of his life. When he looked back on the Christianity he had rejected, his longing for what he had lost was so acute he could not bear to think about it. We have no way of knowing how many people have been swayed from faith in God by the false assumptions of Darwinian evolution posing as settled science, but we know that the resulting state of mind of those who fall cannot be good. As we will see in this chapter, Darwinian evolution promotes atheism, and atheism lacks the power to bestow peace, happiness, meaning, purpose, or hope.

Darwinists want us to believe that atheism frees us from the morality that imposes needless restrictions on our pleasures. But what it actually does is take the heart out of our pleasures by rendering them meaningless. And it does much worse. By removing God from our lives, atheism undermines justice, mercy, honor, and truth. Not only does meaning and happiness disappear, we also lose any basis for believing in traditional morality, and thus our motivation for a life of virtue disappears.

In his book *The Abolition of Man*, the English author and theologian C. S. Lewis expressed the futility of the attempt to subvert faith in God and yet to expect people to remain moral and behave virtuously: "We make men without chests and expect of them virtue and enterprise. We laugh at honor and are shocked to find traitors in our midst. We castrate and bid the geldings be fruitful."[3] Atheism destroys everything that leads to true happiness. The belief that we are beloved creatures of a Creator God, on the other hand, fills our lives with everything we need for meaning, fulfillment, hope, and true purpose.

................................................................

*Darwinists want us to believe that atheism frees us from the morality that imposes needless restrictions on our pleasures. But what it actually does is take the heart out of our pleasures by rendering them meaningless.*

................................................................

### A LEADING ATHEIST FOLLOWS THE ARGUMENT

When the renowned British philosopher and atheist Anthony Flew announced that he had changed his mind and decided there is a God after all, the news made headlines around the world. For more than half a century Flew had been one of the world's most outspoken adversaries of religion. As the author of thirty books, including *God and Philosophy* and *The Presumption of Atheism*, he was also one of the most prolific and persuasive spokesmen for the atheist worldview.

As a young man and junior tutor at Oxford, Flew was acquainted with C. S. Lewis. He presented his first important paper, "Theology and Falsification," before the Socratic Club Lewis chaired at that time. More recent, he has participated in debates with Christian philosophers such as Alvin Plantinga, Ralph McInerny, and William Lane Craig before crowds of as many as seven thousand at a time.

Early in his academic career, Flew made a calculated decision to follow Plato's counsel from *The Republic*, in which Socrates said emphatically, "We must follow the argument wherever it leads." Flew felt certain that neither philosophy nor science would ever prove the existence of a supreme being, and that's what it would take to convince him that God is real.

But then something happened. In the closing decades of the twentieth century, science began moving in new directions. The theory of Intelligent Design was emerging with new and more powerful tools. For the first time Flew realized that the irreducible complexity of life is, in fact, a powerful argument for an intelligent First Cause. He studied the literature and looked carefully at the findings of the biologists, and, true to his convictions, he followed the argument. By the spring of 2004 he had come to the conclusion that the evidence for a superior Mind was too great to ignore.

It was at the outset of a public debate at New York University in May 2004 that he broke the news of his conversion. He wasn't ready just yet to accept the claims of Christianity or Judaism or any of the "revealed religions," he said, but he was convinced that God does exist and is the Creator of life. Flew explained to a stunned audience that he had come to a long-considered logical conclusion, "almost entirely because of the DNA investigations." He said, "What I think the DNA material has done is that it has shown, by the almost unbelievable complexity of the arrangements which are needed to produce [life], that intelligence must have been involved in getting these extraordinarily diverse elements to work together."[4] Flew went on to say, "I now believe that the universe was brought into existence by an infinite Intelligence. I believe that this universe's intricate laws manifest what scientists called the Mind of God. I believe that life and reproduction originate in a divine Source."[5]

Flew's paradigm had not changed. His paradigm was still to follow the argument wherever it leads. Scientific investigation turned him around by showing him a universe that could not have come into existence through naturalistic causes alone. If nothing else, probability theory showed that the odds of that were much too great. After that, he was impressed by the precision and regularity of the laws of nature, by the purposeful organization of life, and, not least, by the fact that such an incredibly complex universe exists at all. The theistic view fit reality, whereas the atheistic view did not. That was enough to seal the deal.[6]

Predictably, atheists were livid that Flew had changed his mind. They said he was a traitor to the cause. Some called him an apostate—he had deserted the faith of the unbeliever—while others said he was being exploited by Christians. The humanist Paul Kurtz claimed Flew hadn't even written his newest book, *There Is a God*, but merely signed off on a ghostwritten job.[7] The fact is, Flew says, he had simply discovered answers that made a great deal more sense than the atheist's creed of nihilistic rejection he once believed.

## THE TRAGIC VIEW OF LIFE

The creed of nihilistic rejection that defines the atheist's worldview is a somber affair. Sometimes described as "the tragic view of life," it is the view that man exists in a silent and uncaring universe, without God and without moral laws, where virtue is always only a matter of personal choice and where the life and death of any person is meaningless except in a purely biological sense.

Darwin certainly shared this perspective, but in deference to public opinion and the pleas of his Christian wife, he attempted in several places in *The Origin of Species* to soften the blow. In the concluding lines of the first edition he wrote, "There is grandeur in this view of life, with its several powers, having been originally breathed into a few forms or into one; and that, whilst this planet has gone cycling on according to the fixed law of gravity, from so simple a beginning endless forms most beautiful and most wonderful have been, and are being, evolved."[8]

But we can only wonder what sort of grandeur he had in mind.

The idea that life on earth evolved by chance, that the world and everything in it is simply a cosmic accident, that humans are merely an intermediary stage between primates and the next level of adaptation, and that life is an endless and pointless struggle for survival without meaning or purpose, ending in annihilation, is hardly the kind of grandeur most people think of first. But this is the default position of modern neo-Darwinism.

In his book *River Out of Eden*, Richard Dawkins tells us that humans are simply "survival machines," equipped by their biology to propagate and pass on their DNA to the next generation. Life is a "replication bomb," he says, meaning presumably that the only value of our kind—or any species, for that matter—is our capacity to reproduce and keep the endless and apparently pointless evolutionary cycle going. Happiness and personal fulfillment have no place in such a view.

Later in the same book, Dawkins admits as much:

This is not a recipe for happiness. So long as DNA is passed on, it does not matter who or what gets hurt in the process. . . . Genes don't care about suffering, because they don't care about anything. . . . This is one of the hardest lessons for humans to learn. We cannot admit that things might be neither good nor evil, neither cruel nor kind, but simply callous—indifferent to all suffering, lacking all purpose.[9]

# THE DEATH OF EVOLUTION

Meaninglessness, lack of purpose, indifference to suffering—these common themes are apparently enough for the evolutionary atheist. How very different from the attitude of hope and joyful anticipation of the Christian worldview. But sadly, as Cornell University historian and evolutionist William B. Provine wrote, there is no room for joy or hope in the atheist's worldview:

> The implications of modern science, however, are clearly inconsistent with most religious traditions. No purposive principles exist in nature. Organic evolution has occurred by various combinations of random genetic drift, natural selection, Mendelian heredity, and many other purposeless mechanisms. Humans are complex organic machines that die completely with no survival of soul or psyche. Humans and other animals make choices frequently, but these are determined by the interaction of heredity and environment and are not the result of free will. No inherent moral or ethical laws exist, nor are there absolute guiding principles for human society. The universe cares nothing for us and we have no ultimate meaning in life.[10]

It can be shocking to witness the utter darkness and hopelessness of such a philosophy, but these views are not at all exceptional—they are fundamental components of the worldview that proponents of Darwinian evolution have been teaching to young people in the public schools and universities for the last half century and longer. And we wonder why there is so much emptiness, unhappiness, and hopelessness among members of the younger generation today.

*Meaninglessness, lack of purpose, indifference to suffering—these common themes are apparently enough for the evolutionary atheist. How very different from the attitude of hope and joyful anticipation of the Christian worldview.*

### THE DARWINIAN ENDORSEMENT OF DEATH

Charles Darwin most certainly held these views as well, and said as much in several places. He believed that death, not life, was the real engine of creativity in the biosphere. After reading the writings of Thomas Malthus, who argued that population growth was a hindrance to human progress, Darwin revised the original manuscript of *The Descent of Man* to draw attention to the importance of limiting humanitarian aid to the sick, the feeble, and the destitute.[11] He said:

We civilised men do our utmost to check the process of elimination; we build asylums for the imbecile, the maimed, and the sick. . . . There is reason to believe that vaccination has preserved thousands. . . . Thus the weak members of civilised societies propagate their kind. No one who has attended to the breeding of domestic animals will doubt that this must be highly injurious to the race of man. It is surprising how soon a want of care, or care wrongly directed, leads to the degeneration of a domestic race; but excepting in the case of man itself, hardly any one is so ignorant as to allow his worst animals to breed.[12]

As the researcher and biographer Benjamin Wiker pointed out, these ideas, published anonymously by Malthus at the end of the eighteenth century, not only confirmed Darwin's cold and unsympathetic view but allowed him to cast death in a whole new light.

Life was profligate, imprudently overproducing, casting forth far more than it could ever feed, generating every manner of variation of species, with no thought about how to care for them all. But death was a good accountant; it knew how to deal with "too much life.". . . Death, Darwin thought, was the key to life.[13]

For the Christian, death is the enemy, the tragic result of sin and mankind's fall from grace. But for Darwin, as Wiker concluded, "death was, is, and always will be, the creator."[14] This heartless view also became the justification for the eugenics movement popularized by Darwin's cousin, Francis Galton, and later carried out with such terrible efficiency by the Nazis in wartime Germany and by the abortion lobbyists in America today. The founder of Planned Parenthood, Margaret Sanger, described her mission as ridding society of "human weeds."[15] The slaughter of innocents that she began is now well past the fifty million mark in this country alone.[16]

## Death: An End or a Beginning?

Charles Darwin's view of death was cold, calculating, and inhumane, as one might expect from a man who had lost his faith in God and had no hope of life beyond the grave. Several historians have pointed out that Darwin's loss of faith may be linked to the death of his nine-year-old daughter Annie in 1851. Annie was an exceptional child and clearly his favorite, but nothing Charles or his wealthy, medically sophisticated, and socially well-connected family could do was enough. She lingered in a miserable state for many weeks, with Darwin at her side much of the time, and no expense was spared to save her. When Annie died, his biographers tell us, Darwin lost all confidence in the possibility of a divine and compassionate Creator.

"From that moment on," the English biographers White and Gribbin reported, "Darwin was a total, uncompromising atheist: his only god was rationality, his only saviour, logic and science; to that end he would continue to dedicate his life. There was no meaning to existence other than a culmination of biological events. Life was selfish and cruel, headless and heartless. Beyond biology there was nothing."[17] For Darwin, death was the end of everything.

To escape the pain of his loss, Darwin poured himself into his work and remained in his study for endless hours, and even slept there for weeks at a time. His wife and teenaged daughters looked after him and served his meals separately while he spent countless hours examining saltwater barnacles in his makeshift laboratory, in hopes of discovering some tangible evidence, however small, of adaptation and transmutation. He never found it, just as he never found any convincing proof of any of his theories during his lifetime.

Perhaps no one has expressed the heartbreaking emptiness of the atheist's view of death as poignantly as the nineteenth-century American atheist and orator Robert Ingersoll. At the graveside of a brother who died unexpectedly, he said:

> Whether in mid-sea or among the breakers of the farther shore, a wreck must mark at last the end of each and all. And every life, no matter if its every hour is rich with love and every moment jeweled with joy, will, at its close, become a tragedy, as sad and deep and dark as can be woven of warp and woof, of mystery and death. . . . Life is a narrow vale between the cold and barren peak of two eternities. We strive in vain to look beyond the heights. We cry aloud, and the only answer is the echo of our wailing cry. From the voiceless lips of the unreplying dead there comes no word.[18]

As Ingersoll's lament shows, the greatest sorrow for those who share this morbid philosophy is not only the death of a loved one but the impossibility of consolation and the utter lack of hope. Like Darwin, Ingersoll saw death as the end, with nothing beyond but an empty void of oblivion. The tragic irony is that the atheist's philosophy is also wrong. Science has not disproved the existence of God, nor can it. There is life beyond the grave.

## C. S. Lewis on Meaning and Purpose

Death was also a major obstacle in the life of the author and apologist C. S. Lewis, who turned to atheism after the death of his mother when he was just nine years old. In his autobiography, *Surprised by Joy*, Lewis wrote, "With my mother's death all settled happiness disappeared from my life. There was much fun, many pleasures, many stabs of joy; but no more of the old security. It was sea and islands now; the great continent had sunk like Atlantis."[19]

Without his mother or the support of a profoundly depressed and emotionally absent father, Lewis turned away from God, unable to put his trust in a Creator who would allow such misery to exist. And he discovered there were many other reasons not to believe—the problem of evil, for example; the odd similarities between Bible stories and the fairy tales he enjoyed as a child; the seeming impossibility of the miracles in the Bible; and the fact that his prayers were never answered.

These were insurmountable obstacles for Lewis, and in his atheist rebellion during his student days he was highly vocal and ruthless in his assault on the naive assumptions of Christians. Like many atheists, he decided the problem of evil and the experience of pain and suffering were undeniable proofs that God was either not there at all or, if he was there, he was a tyrant not to be admired.

But unlike Darwin, Lewis did not shut down his mind and refuse to consider evidence that confronted his atheism. His railings against religion and the lack of meaning in the world brought him face to face with another dilemma. As Lewis explained in *Mere Christianity:*

> My argument against God was that the universe seemed so cruel and unjust. But how had I got this idea of *just* and *unjust*? A man does not call a line crooked unless he has some idea of a straight line. What was I comparing this universe with when I called it unjust? . . . Thus, in the very act of trying to prove that God did not exist—in other words, that the whole of reality was senseless—I found I was forced to assume that one part of reality—namely my idea of justice—was full of sense.[20]

Before long Lewis reached the conclusion that the self-serving answers of atheism were too simple. If the universe has no meaning, as he had once thought, then how was he able to recognize that it has no meaning? If there were no light in the universe and, therefore, no need for creatures with eyes, how would they know it was dark? *Dark*, he said, would be a word with no meaning. And if justice were simply a meaningless term, why did he feel such sorrow and longing when it seemed to be missing?

By the end of this emotional journey, Lewis came to the conclusion that God must actually exist and must have created a world in which concepts such as justice and right and wrong are worth pursuing. It would be some time before he took the next step, to become a follower of Jesus Christ, but he had turned an important corner.

Gradually, through the process of rational thought, Lewis had come to the conclusion that suffering and loss are a natural part of human existence brought about by mankind's conscious rebellion against God. The fall from grace affected not only the fate and well-being of mankind but the creation as well. God said to Adam:

> Cursed is the ground for your sake;
> in toil you shall eat of it
> all the days of your life.
> Both thorns and thistles it shall bring forth for you.[21]

Men had brought about their own demise through faithlessness, but the resurrection provided a means of healing and restoration for all who would believe.

# THE DEATH OF EVOLUTION

Like Anthony Flew, Lewis followed the evidence with an open mind and found intellectually satisfying answers to the problem of pain and death that trip up so many and cast them into unbelief. He found a rational faith that explained reality rather than falling into the meaningless and despairing void of atheism. He learned the truth about death: it is not the end.

Death brings sadness for the Christian, as it does for everyone, but those who cherish the gospel message have the confidence of knowing that death is not the end. While it is never easy to lose a loved one, the sadness we feel at the graveside of Christian relatives and friends is not shattering because we know what comes next. Death is a transformation, a new beginning. This was Paul's message to the believers at Corinth: "If in this life only we have hope in Christ, we are of all men the most pitiable," he said. "But now Christ is risen from the dead, and has become the firstfruits of those who have fallen asleep. For . . . in Christ all shall be made alive."[22]

*Death brings sadness for the Christian, as it does for everyone, but those who cherish the gospel message have the confidence of knowing that death is not the end.*

This truth is "the blessed hope" of the believer. Unlike Darwin's feeble attempt at whistling past the graveyard, there actually is "grandeur in this view of life." The tragic irony is that the atheistic philosophy of death is dead wrong. In the resurrection of Christ, we have absolute assurance that there is life beyond the grave.

### THE RATIONALITY OF BELIEF IN GOD

Richard Dawkins complained in his book *The God Delusion* that if God is truly omnipresent and omnipotent, capable of creating the universe, why hasn't he left some evidence of himself in it? Here again, the question is an admission of the writer's profound ignorance of what Christians actually believe. Throughout Scripture, from beginning to end, we are reminded of how the majesty of the creation gives eloquent testimony, not only to the inevitable fact of a Creator, but also to his character. This is expressed nowhere better than in the Psalms where David exclaimed:

> The heavens declare the glory of God;
>> And the firmament shows His handiwork.
> Day unto day utters speech,
>> And night unto night reveals knowledge.
> There is no speech nor language
>> Where their voice is not heard.
> Their line has gone out through all the earth,
>> And their words to the end of the world.
> In them He has set a tabernacle for the sun.[23]

# THE DEATH OF EVOLUTION

Throughout the Bible we have numerous accounts of people acknowledging the immanence and accessibility of God even though they could not see him in physical form. In many places in the New Testament, Paul reminds believers of the immanence and majesty of God but also stresses the fact that, through faith in Jesus Christ, every believer has access to the throne of God. Although God is infinitely wise and powerful, he is nevertheless accessible. Paul wrote in Acts 17:

> God, who made the world and everything in it, since He is Lord of heaven and earth, does not dwell in temples made with hands. Nor is He worshiped with men's hands, as though He needed anything, since He gives to all life, breath, and all things. And He has made from one blood every nation of men to dwell on all the face of the earth, and has determined their preappointed times and the boundaries of their dwellings, so that they should seek the Lord, in the hope that they might grope for Him and find Him, though He is not far from each one of us.[24]

Both the Old and New Testaments affirm that God is immortal, invisible, immutable, and self-existent. He is not a created being and is not therefore subject to the laws of nature. He created those laws, and all of nature and the cosmos adhere to them. God the Creator is outside time and space and cannot be proved or disproved by science, but he has given us a record of himself in the testimony of the prophets and apostles and, most important, through the life, death, and resurrection of his Son.

The Bible teaches that Jesus willingly stepped out of eternity and took on the form of a man in order to redeem all those who willingly receive him. This is not a hard gospel, but it requires an act of faith. Just days before his trial and crucifixion, Jesus said of himself, "the Son of Man did not come to be served, but to serve, and to give His life a ransom for many."[25] No other sacrifice could atone for the sinfulness of man. The life and death of God's only Son was, and still is, the ultimate gift of life. But, in his egotism and intellectual arrogance, the atheist willingly rejects this free gift.

................................................................................

*"Suspicions about Darwin's theory arise for two reasons. The first: the theory makes little sense. The second: it is supported by little evidence."*

—DR. DAVID BERLINSKI, mathematician and philosopher,
featured in the film *Expelled*[26]

................................................................................

Fortunately, not all men and women of science are so blind. As we have seen in previous chapters, more and more scientists are coming to see that the Christian worldview does not limit science, but actually makes it stronger and more rewarding. The Nobel Prize-winning physicist Charles Townes eloquently expressed the logic of this view, affirming that, "Faith is necessary for the scientist even to get started, and deep faith necessary for him to carry out his tougher tasks. Why? Because he must have confidence that there is order in the universe and that the human mind—in fact his own mind—has a good chance of understanding this order."[27]

Dr. Owen Gingerich, emeritus astronomer at the Smithsonian Astrophysical Observatory and former research professor of astronomy and the history of science at Harvard, says much the same in his 2003 book *God's Universe*, where he wrote, "To me, belief in a final cause, a Creator-God, gives a coherent understanding of why the universe seems so congenially designed for the existence of intelligent, self-reflective life." Further, as he told an audience of scientists and academics at a 2003 conference in New Hampshire, we each come to our worldview, "not by proofs but by persuasion, by the coherence of the picture we construct of the world and our place in it."[28]

In terms that even the least religiously inclined ought to understand, Gingerich said, "I cannot prove the existence of a designing Creator any more than I can solve the problem of evil. I am simply personally persuaded that an intentionally created universe, with one of its likely purposes the emergence of conscious and self-contemplative intelligence, makes sense to me, is satisfyingly coherent, and is persuasive."[29] Such a view is not only vastly more rewarding than the dispirited philosophy of contemporary atheism, it is the one view that actually makes sense of the mystery of life.

# RESTORING MEANING AND PURPOSE

## EVOLUTION EXPOSED

When we look at Charles Darwin objectively, we cannot get around the fact that he was not the genius that secular science has made him out to be. He was not even a scientist by our standards. His only university-level training was two ill-spent years in medical college, which he left early without a diploma, and three years at Cambridge culminating in a modest pretheology degree. In fact, he spent most of his time at Cambridge looking for ways to amuse himself and rarely attended lectures until his final term.

His voyage on the HMS *Beagle* started as a lark, escaping from the prospect of spending the rest of his life as a small-town vicar preaching a gospel he no longer believed. In fact, he could not have become a minister without additional training and an ordination hearing that, more than likely, he could not have passed.

Charles Darwin was never more than an amateur naturalist. He would gladly have spent the rest of his life as a sporting man—a fact he had confessed in his journals—enjoying the luxuries his inherited wealth provided. His father despaired more than once of his ever finding a suitable profession and feared the *Beagle* adventure would be his ruin. But the specimens he sent home to Henslow and Sedgwick made him famous, and the rest of what he accomplished was the product of an overzealous imagination and relentless self-promotion.

Yet, for all that, Darwinian evolution turns out to be a shallow and unsubstantiated belief system propagated by men and women

141

whose commitment to a godless worldview far exceeds their belief in the credibility of Darwin's conclusions.

Dr. Colin Reeves, professor of information sciences at Coventry University in Great Britain, offered a stark assessment:

> Darwinism was an interesting idea in the nineteenth century, when handwaving explanations gave a plausible if not properly scientific framework into which we could fit biological facts. However, what we have learned since the days of Darwin throws doubt on natural selection's ability to create complex biological systems—and we still have little more than handwaving as an argument in its favour.[30]

Christopher Williams, a professor of biochemistry at Ohio State University, expressed a similar view.

> Few people outside of genetics or biochemistry realize that evolutionists still can provide no substantive details at all about the origin of life, and particularly the origin of genetic information in the first self-replicating organism. What genes did it require—or did it even have genes? How much DNA and RNA did it have—or did it even have nucleic acids? How did huge information-rich molecules arise before natural selection? Exactly how did the genetic code linking nucleic acids to amino acid sequence originate? Clearly the origin of life—the foundation of evolution—is still virtually all speculation, and little or no fact.[31]

And, finally, the mathematician and philosopher David Berlinski, who has written and spoken with brilliance and candor about the failures of evolutionary theory, said,

> Unable to say what evolution has accomplished, biologists now find themselves unable to say whether evolution has accomplished it. This leaves evolutionary theory in the doubly damned position of having compromised the concepts needed to make sense of life— complexity, adaptation, design—while simultaneously conceding that the theory does little to explain them.[32]

These are problems that cannot be ignored. But there are other problems as well. To begin with, many of Darwin's statements in *The Origin of Species* and elsewhere are false, based on theory and wishful thinking rather than science. In the final chapter of the book, where Darwin attempts to quickly lay to rest the criticisms of his more accomplished peers, he wrote, "If we admit that the geological record is imperfect to an extreme degree, then the facts, which the record does give, strongly support the theory of descent with modification. New species have come on the stage slowly and at successive intervals; and the amount of change, after equal intervals of time, is widely different in different groups."[33]

Unfortunately, there is nothing in the fossil record to support this view. While the idea of species emerging "slowly and at successive intervals" fits nicely with the theory, the geological record is devoid of emerging species except the one sudden burst of new life called the Cambrian explosion. But Darwin continued with his false assumption, saying, "When I view all beings not as special creations, but as the lineal descendants of some few beings which lived long before the first bed of the Cambrian system was deposited, they seem to me to become ennobled. Judging from the past, we may safely infer that not one living species will transmit its unaltered likeness to a distant futurity."[34]

Again, the theory doesn't work. While no one disputes that species can adapt to their environment in small and beneficial ways over time, there is no evidence, either in the fossil record or any biological form, of the kinds of transformation Darwin describes. It's true there have been innumerable hoaxes over the years, perpetrated by unethical and ambitious scientists trying to fabricate such evidence—Piltdown Man, Nebraska Man, the Archaeoraptor, Ernst Haeckel's fraudulent drawings of fetal development, to name a few—but after 150 years of ardent search for an authentic transitional form, the theory has come up empty.

## THE DAMAGE IN DARWIN'S WAKE

Shortly before noon, November 7, 2007, eighteen-year-old Pekka-Eric Auvinen entered a Finnish high school armed with a semi-automatic pistol. Immediately he began shooting. By the time the bloody spree ended, he had killed eight people and wounded twelve others before firing a bullet into his own head.

The multiple videos and writings police found in Auvinen's home left no ambiguity about his motivations. They revealed that he did not believe in God. He believed that everything is the product of mindless evolution, and that existence has no purpose. From among his writings and videos emerged these telling statements: "It's time to put natural selection and survival of the fittest back on track. . . . There are no other universal laws than the laws of nature and the laws of physics. . . . I'm the dictator of my own life."[35]

*While no one disputes that species can adapt to their environment in small and beneficial ways over time, there is no evidence, either in the fossil record or any biological form, of the kinds of transformation Darwin describes.*

No one would claim that all who hold atheistic and evolutionary beliefs are likely to commit mass murders. Yet the meaninglessness that is implicit in Darwinism almost always leads to the less visible but equally real tragedy of personal despair, just as it did for John Romanes, Robert Ingersoll, and Darwin himself. When despair breeds desperation, there is nothing in Darwinism to provide the counterbalance of a moral code to keep those harmful impulses in check. Ideas do have consequences. One's theology—or the lack of it—will ultimately dictate one's behavior, as it did with devastating results for Darwinian adherents such as Josef Stalin and Adolf Hitler. What one does will be drawn from the well of what one believes.

Witnessing the great harm, both societal and personal, that has been done by Darwinism over the years, it is difficult for men and women of faith to deny the resentment and disappointment we feel in the persistence of its adherents in pushing an unproved, intellectually and spiritually void theory on the rest of us. Instead of rejoicing in the beauty and majesty of our world, praising God for the creation and our place on this "privileged planet," the evolutionist paints a dismal picture drawn entirely from the darkness of his own imagination, and then projects that monstrous misrepresentation onto the world. The Christian has no reason to fear this false portrait. Christians are not afraid of what the atheist can do; rather, we fear for the atheist, for the choices he has made, and for the eternity he has chosen.

Thirty years ago, an American atheist and freelance writer penned this bitter assessment of the goal of Darwinian evolution:

Christianity has fought, still fights, and will fight science to the desperate end over evolution, because evolution destroys utterly and finally the very reason Jesus's earthly life was supposedly made necessary. Destroy Adam and Eve and the original sin, and in the rubble you will find the sorry remains of the Son of God.

If Jesus was not the redeemer who died for our sins, and this is what evolution means, then Christianity is nothing.[36]

Such thoughts can only come from men and women whose addiction to sin is vastly greater than their powers of reason. The man who dives headlong from a fifty-foot tower claiming the law of gravity is a fraud will suffer precisely the same fate as the man who slips and falls accidentally to his death. Merely denying the resurrection power of the Son of God does no harm to Christ's message or to Christianity; but how many lives have been lost for eternity because of the lies put forth in the name of atheistic evolution? For this the Christian justifiably weeps, and this is the real damage that Darwin's absurd theory has done.

The anger that comes from the mouths of atheists—and from books written by Dawkins, Hitchens, Harris, Dennett, Stenger, and all the rest—are signs that Darwin's flawed theory is in serious disarray. The new science of Intelligent Design, perhaps better than anything else at present, has begun the process of stripping away evolution's false front, and this is why they rage.

The dictatorship of Darwinism is about to run its course. Over the past 150 years, untold millions have been snared by its pretensions, and millions more have lost not only their faith but their hope of a life worth living. But things are changing. For the time being, the schools and colleges still have locks on their doors—the last thing they want now is for light to seep into the debate. But in time the truth will emerge, and no one will be able to ignore the damage Mr. Darwin's little theory has done.

The good news is that there is a God and he is not silent. There is a Creator who made the world, a Creator who made it possible for us to communicate with him, and, through simple faith, to find answers to life's most challenging questions. As more and more of us come to recognize this truth, the schools and colleges, and perhaps even the philosophy of science will have to change. And who knows where that could lead?

# EPILOGUE

The great tragedy of Darwinism is the damage it has inflicted by causing an untold number of people to miss out on the eternal blessings of knowing God. But it has also taken its toll on the Christian faith. Many Christians, influenced by the prevalence of the theory in the media, universities, government, and the scientific community, have felt genuinely conflicted about their beliefs. When continually bombarded by claims made in the name of science that undermine religion, it's easy to wonder whether our religious beliefs are as trustworthy as we at first thought. Some Christians may begin to make compromises or simply keep quiet about their true convictions in order to avoid embarrassment.

One of the motivations for this book has been to remove the sense of discomfort believers feel in these situations. While the defenders of evolution will no doubt continue to characterize the struggle as a battle between science and religion, true science and true religion can never be in conflict. The God who created the universe is the Author of both. The real battle is between truth and falsehood. And, as we have seen throughout these pages, falsehood is the only reasonable way to characterize the Darwinian hypothesis.

No proof has ever been found for the fundamental principles of the theory. Furthermore, evolution offers no basis for morality, meaning, or hope. We can't help but wonder how a theory that so consistently conflicts with our experience of reality, that offers no confirming proof, and leads ultimately to meaninglessness and despair can continue to hold such a firm grasp on contemporary culture. The only explanation, as some of its adherents have candidly admitted, is the evolutionists' desire to remove God from the equation in order to live a life without moral restraints—which is such a shallow and self-defeating goal.

On the other hand, believers can find encouragement in recent studies by a growing number of influential scientists that show living organisms, down to the tiniest cells, demonstrate an irreducible complexity that defies evolutionary gradualism. The new findings tell us that life must be the product of an Intelligent Designer. Together, the weaknesses of Darwin's hypothesis and the solid evidence for creation by an Intelligent Designer ought to give us ample reason to declare with certainty that there is a God who is the Creator and Sustainer of all there is.

# EPILOGUE

Affirming this truth boldly is not a meaningless exercise. There is great need for believers to take a stand to counter the claims of Darwinism, declaring that meaning, morality, and hope are possible when we acknowledge that we were created by God for the purpose of reflecting his nature. This declaration may take many forms. We can affirm our beliefs with boldness in the classroom, in discussions with our friends and coworkers, and in the public arena whenever traditional morality faces legal challenges. We can affirm with our voices and our votes our opposition to the degenerating side-effects of Darwinism as they are now being pushed politically in the form of abortion, euthanasia, embryonic stem cell research, same-sex marriage, and the endorsement of alternative lifestyles.

We can have confidence and boldness when we know we have no reason to doubt. That's when our faith is most exhilarating. With the certainty of God's truth as our foundation, we are free to embrace the doctrines of our faith wholeheartedly and with a boldness that cannot be shaken by spurious claims masquerading as science. This intellectual assurance of faith is a fine thing, indeed, and if that were all we gained from exposing the vapidity of evolution and the rationality of creation, we would be grateful. But there's more. Confidence in the truth of God as Creator not only gives us intellectual assurance, it can bring real joy. The truth can overflow our minds and fill our hearts.

# EPILOGUE

Consider, for example, those summer nights when you've stretched out on the lawn and gazed into the star-studded mystery of deep space. Think of the ways you process what you see. First, think of yourself as a Darwinian evolutionist. With this mindset you will see the stars as accidental accumulations of burning gases. You will see the occasional comet streaking across the night sky as random trash flung into space by mindless, mechanical forces. None of what you see has any real meaning or purpose. The universe exploded blindly into existence and will burn out in oblivion, leaving nothing at all—not even a memory. You are alone in the universe. You have no value at all. You are a momentary flash appearing out of nowhere and fading into nothing. All existence is bleak, meaningless, and without purpose.

In stark contrast, consider looking into the same universe as a believer in the Creator God. You see the stars not as mechanical and accidental blobs of burning gases, but as works of awe-inspiring art, breathtakingly beautiful and incredibly intricate. You feel awe at the immense creativity and power of a Supreme Being who could conceive such glory and breathe it into existence. You realize that nothing you see is accidental or purposeless. It has all been formed and held in place by a complex matrix of laws that regulate energy and maintain order, all ordained and sustained by a loving Creator.

The resemblance between the words cosmos and cosmetic

is no accident. Some of the ancients called the universe "God's ornament," recognizing it not only as a masterpiece of precision and design, but also of immense beauty. Believers who are confident in their beliefs can see the cosmos as the ancients did— as an eloquent expression of a Creator God who delights not only in order and functional design, but also in sheer beauty.

The awe you feel in the presence of such a massive display of power and beauty becomes even greater when you realize that you were created by the same hand that formed the galaxies. God has shown how precious we are to him by giving us this beautiful cosmos where we can revel in the beauty of his creation. He has also paid us the enormous compliment of creating us in his image and placing us in the world to be his agents, as representatives of his character, truth, and love. This is a worldview that gives our lives immense purpose and meaning.

As if that were not enough, the Creator demonstrated just how dear we are to him in the stupendous price he paid so he would not have to spend eternity without us. If the universe is God's ornament, clearly he sees us as the priceless jewels that adorn that ornament. Indeed, the love he has for us is greater by far than the immense wonder of the cosmos. What a monumental gift can be ours when we affirm God as our loving Creator and place our lives confidently in his hands.

# NOTES

*Introduction*

1. Owen Gingerich, *God's Universe* (Cambridge, MA: Harvard University Press, 2006), 12.
2. After more than thirty years of speculation on his findings, Darwin wrote to the distinguished English botanist Joseph Hooker describing his ideas concerning the beginnings of organic life. He said, "It is often said that all the conditions for the first production of a living organism are now present, which could ever have been present. But if (and oh! what a big if!) we could conceive in some warm little pond, with all sorts of ammonia and phosphoric salts, light, heat, electricity, &c., present, that a proteine compound was chemically formed ready to undergo still more complex changes, at the present day such matter would be instantly absorbed, which would not have been the case before living creatures were found." Charles Darwin to Joseph Hooker, in *The Life and Letters of Charles Darwin,* ed. Francis Darwin (New York: Appleton, 1911), 2:202–03.
3. William B. Provine, from his 1998 Darwin Day address "Evolution: Free Will and Punishment and Meaning in Life,"

# NOTES

http://eeb.bio.utk.edu/darwin/Archives/1998ProvineAbstract.htm.

4. Isaiah 44:24–25.

*Chapter One*

1. Malcolm Muggeridge, *The End of Christendom* (Grand Rapids, MI: Eerdmans, 1980), 59.

2. Pew Research Center for the People and the Press, "Public Praises Science; Scientists Fault Public, Media," July 9, 2009, http://people-press.org/report/528/.

3. Richard Morin, "Can We Believe In Polls About God?" *Washington Post*, June 1, 1998, http://www.washingtonpost.com/wp-srv/politics/polls/wat/archive/wat060198.htm.

4. Pew Research Center, "Public Praises Science."

5. Richard Dawkins, *The Greatest Show on Earth: The Evidence for Evolution* (New York: Free Press, 2009), 429–31.

6. Martin Beckford, "Children Are Born Believers in God, Academic Claims," *Telegraph* (UK), Nov. 24, 2008, http://www.telegraph.co.uk/news/newstopics/religion/3512686/Children-are-born-believers-in-God-academic-claims.html.

7. Ibid.

8. Ibid.

9. Michael Brooks, "Born Believers: How Your Brain Creates God," *New Scientist* 2694, February 4, 2009, http://www.newscientist.com/article/mg20126941.700-born-believers-how-your-brain-creates-god.html.

10. Ibid.

11. Dawkins, *The Greatest Show on Earth*, 435–36.

12. Ibid., 85.

13. Richard Dawkins, review of Donald Johanson and Maitland Edey's "Blueprint," in *New York Times*, sec. 7, April 9, 1989.

14. Paul Davies, *The Goldilocks Enigma: Why Is the Universe Just Right for Life?* (New York: Mariner Books, 2008). Also, in the

concluding statement of the book *The Cosmic Blueprint,* Paul Davies emphasizes the extraordinary fine-tuning of the universe, saying: "The very fact that the universe is creative, and that the laws have permitted complex structures to emerge and develop to the point of consciousness—in other words, that the universe has organized its own self-awareness—is for me powerful evidence that there is 'something going on' behind it all. The impression of design is overwhelming. Science may explain all the processes whereby the universe evolves its own destiny, but that still leaves room for there to be a meaning behind existence." Paul Davies, *The Cosmic Blueprint: New Discoveries in Nature's Creative Ability to Order the Universe* (New York: Simon & Schuster, 1988), 203.

15. Roger Penrose, *The Emperor's New Mind: Concerning Computers, Minds, and the Laws of Physics* (New York: Oxford University Press, 1989), 445.

16. David Berlinski, "The Deniable Darwin," *Commentary 101,* no. 6, June 1, 1996, http://www.commentarymagazine.com/viewarticle.cfm/the-deniable-darwin-8573. (Subscription required.)

17. John Micklethwait and Adrian Wooldridge, *God Is Back: How the Global Revival of Faith Is Changing the World* (New York: Penguin, 2009), 12.

18. Ibid., 16.

19. Ibid., 159. See also The Pew Forum on Religion and Public Life, "Religious Landscape Survey: June 2008," http://religions.pewforum.org/pdf/report2-religious-landscape-study-full.pdf.

20. Pew Forum, "Religious Landscape Survey."

21. Alister McGrath and Joanna Collicutt McGrath, *The Dawkins Delusion? Atheist Fundamentalism and the Denial of the Divine* (Downers Grove, IL: InterVarsity Press, 2007).

22. Francis S. Collins, *The Language of God: A Scientist Presents Evidence for Belief* (New York: Free Press, 2007), 199–201.

23. Davies, *Goldilocks Enigma.*

24. Michael Behe, *Darwin's Black Box: The Biochemical Challenge to Evolution* (New York: Free Press, 2006), 3–4.

25. In "Part VI: Difficulties of the Theory" under the heading "Modes of Transition," Darwin wrote: "If it could be demonstrated that any complex organ existed which could not possibly have been formed by numerous successive slight modifications, my theory would absolutely break down." Charles Darwin, *The Origin of Species,* Harvard Classics ed. (New York: P. F. Collier & Son, 1909), 185.

26. Denton wrote, "To grasp the reality of life as it has been revealed by molecular biology, we must first magnify a cell a thousand million times until it is 20 kilometers in diameter and resembles a giant airship large enough to cover a great city like London or New York. What we would see then would be an object of unparalleled complexity . . . we would find ourselves in a world of supreme technology and bewildering complexity." Michael Denton, *Evolution: A Theory in Crisis* (Bethesda, MD: Adler & Adler, 1986), 328.

27. Behe, *Darwin's Black Box,* 187–208.

28. Richard Dawkins, "Big Ideas: Evolution," *New Scientist* (September 17, 2005): 33.

29. These accounts of the lives of Galileo and Copernicus are found in Donald DeMarco, "The Dispute Between Galileo and the Catholic Church," *Homiletic & Pastoral Review* 101, no. 3 (May-June 1986): 23–51, 53–59. From the Catholic Education Resource Center, http://www.catholiceducation.org/articles/science/sc0043.html.

30. Richard Tarnas, *The Passion of the Western Mind: Understanding the Ideas That Have Shaped Our World View* (New York: Ballantine, 1991), 252.

31. Dr. Hutchinson is the founder of "The Faith of Great Scientists" seminar at MIT. His comments here were given in a plenary address at the ASA Annual Meeting in 2002.

# NOTES

32. Ibid.
33. Richard H. Bube, "We Believe in Creation," in *Origins and Change: Selected Readings from the Journal of the American Scientific Affiliation* (1978): iii-iv, 1978.
34. Henry F. Schaefer III, *Science and Christianity: Conflict or Coherence?* (Athens, GA: The Apollos Trust, 2003), 175.
35. Ibid., 178.
36. Richard H. Bube, "Towards a Christian View of Science," *Journal of the American Scientific Affiliation* 23 (March 1971): 4.

*Chapter Two*

1. W. R. Thompson, introduction to *Origin of Species* (London: Everyman, 1958).
2. Benjamin Wiker, *The Myth of Darwin* (Washington DC: Regnery, 2009), 4.
3. Michael White and John Gribbin, *Darwin: A Life in Science* (New York: Dutton Group, 1995), 8.
4. Ibid., 12.
5. Wiker, *The Myth of Darwin*, 4.
6. Charles Darwin, *The Autobiography of Charles Darwin, 1809-1822* (New York: W. W. Norton, 1969), 56.
7. Charles Darwin to C. T. Whitley, Letter 148, November 15, 1831. http://darwinproject.ac.uk/entry-148.
8. Wiker, *The Myth of Darwin*, 72.
9. Ernst Mayr, *One Long Argument: Charles Darwin and the Genesis of Modern Evolutionary Thought* (Cambridge, MA: Harvard University Press, 1991), 36–37.
10. G. K. Chesterton, "Doubts about Darwinism," *Illustrated London News*, July 17, 1920. Note also Huxley's comment: "Of moral purpose I see no trace in Nature. That is an article of exclusively human manufacture—and very much to our credit." In Leonard

Huxley, *The Life and Letters of Thomas Henry Huxley* (London: Macmillan, 1900), 2:285.

11. Huxley announced in a public lecture, "I discovered that one of the unpardonable sins . . . is for a man to presume to go about unlabelled. . . . I could find no label that would suit me, so, in my desire to range myself and be respectable, I invented one. . . . I called myself an Agnostic." In Cyril Bibby, *T. H. Huxley: Scientist, Humanist, and Educator* (New York: Horizon, 1960), 60.

12. Charles Darwin to Charles Lyell, October 11, 1859, in *The Life and Letters of Charles Darwin,* ed. Francis Darwin (London: John Murray, 1887), 2:211.

13. Charles Darwin to J. D. Hooker, March 29, 1863, in *The Life and Letters of Charles Darwin,* ed. Francis Darwin (London: John Murray, 1887), 3:18.

14. Wiker, *The Myth of Darwin*, xi.

*Chapter Three*

1. William Lane Craig, "The Indispensability of Meta-Ethical Foundations for Morality," *Foundations* 5 (1997): 9–12.

2. For an important and persuasive discussion of the influence of mere ideas on society, see Dallas Willard, *The Divine Conspiracy* (New York: HarperOne, 1998).

3. It was Charles Darwin's cousin, Francis Galton, who coined the term *eugenics* in 1883 and formed the first societies to control breeding among mental, physical, and racial undesirables in order to preserve the purity of the human race. The founder of Planned Parenthood, Margaret Sanger, was one of the most notable eugenicists of the twentieth century, and made it her calling to help rid society of "illiterates, paupers, unemployables, criminals, prostitutes, dope fiends" and others she described as "human weeds." See also chapter five, note 15.

# NOTES

4. Michael Ruse and E. O. Wilson, "The Evolution of Ethics," in James Huchingson, *Religion and the Natural Sciences: The Range of Engagement* (New York: Harcourt Brace Jovanovich, 1993), 210.

5. John G. West, "Does Darwinism Support Traditional Morality?" Center for Science and Culture, May 1, 2009, http://www .discovery.org/a/9541.

6. Ecclesiastes 2:10–11 (NIV).

7. Benjamin D. Wiker, "Intelligent Design vs. Blind Evolution: The Moral Implications," *New Oxford Review*, March 2001, http://www.newoxfordreview.org/article.jsp?did=0301-wiker. (Registration required.)

8. Richard Lewontin, "Billions and Billions of Demons," *New York Review of Books* (January 9, 1997), 31.

9. Ibid.

10. Aldous Huxley, *Ends and Means* (London: Chatto & Windus, 1937), 273.

11. Jeremy Rifkin, *Entropy: A New World View* (New York: Bantam, 1981), 55.

12. Ibid.

13. Fyodor Dostoevsky, *The Brothers Karamazov*, trans. Andrew R. McAndrew (New York: Bantam, 1970), 95.

14. The study was conducted by sociologists Elaine Howard Ecklund of the University at Buffalo and Christopher P. Scheitle of Pennsylvania State University. For more, see Lee Dye, "The Clash Between Religion and Science," *ABC News*, July 3, 2007, http://abcnews.go.com/Technology/story?id=3341576&page=1.

15. "American Nones: The Profile of the No Religion Population," American Religious Identification Survey 2008, November 2008, http://www.americanreligionsurvey-aris.org/.

16. Ibid.

# NOTES

*Chapter Four*

1. Theodore Roszak, *Unfinished Animal: The Aquarian Frontier and the Evolution of Consciousness* (New York: HarperCollins, 1977), 101–02.

2. Rodney Stark, *The Victory of Reason: How Christianity Led to Freedom, Capitalism, and Western Success* (New York: Random House, 2005), 12.

3. Genesis 1:2.

4. Stark, *Victory of Reason,* 14.

5. Nancy R. Pearcey and Charles B. Thaxton, *The Soul of Science: Christian Faith and Natural Philosophy* (Wheaton, IL: Crossway, 1994), 21.

6. "Science: Semi-Creation," *Time*, May 25, 1953, http://www .time.com/time/magazine/article/0,9171,890596,00.html.

7. Ilya Prigogine, Gregoire Nicolis, and Agnes Babloyants, "Thermodynamics of Evolution," *Physics Today* 25, no. 11 (1972): 23.

8. Dean Kenyon, video interview, "Unlocking the Mysteries," http:// www.youtube.com/watch?v=0ycPJTmQiQM. See also Dean Kenyon and Percival W. Davis, *Of Pandas and People: The Central Question of Biological Origins* (Dallas, TX: Houghton Mifflin, 1993).

9. Ibid.

10. Lee Strobel, *The Case for Faith* (Philadelphia: Running Press, 2000), 98.

11. Darwin, *Origin of Species,* 181. (See chap. 1, n. 25.)

12. William Paley, *Natural Theology: or, Evidences of the Existence and Attributes of the Deity, Collected from the Appearances of Nature,* 12th ed. (London: J. Faulder, 1809).

13. Ray Bohlin, review, "Expelled: No Intelligence Allowed," Probe, March 20, 2008, http://www.probe.org/site/c.fdKEIMNsEoG/ b.4217879/k.48BD/Expelled_No_Intelligence_Allowed.htm.

# NOTES

14. I. L. Cohen, *Darwin Was Wrong: A Study in Probabilities* (New York: New Research Publications, 1984), 213–14.

15. Jerry Bergman, *Slaughter of the Dissidents* (Seattle: Leafcutter Press, 2008).

*Chapter Five*

1. Robert Jastrow, *God and the Astronomers* (New York: Readers Library, 1992), 106–07.

2. George John Romanes, *Thoughts on Religion* (Chicago: Open Court, 1895), 29.

3. C. S. Lewis, *The Abolition of Man* (New York: HarperOne, 1974), 26.

4. Anthony Flew, *There Is a God: How the World's Most Notorious Atheist Changed His Mind* (New York: HarperOne, 2007), 66–67.

5. Ibid., 75.

6. Ibid., 155.

7. Mark Oppenheimer, "The Turning of an Atheist," *New York Times*, Nov. 4, 2007, http://www.nytimes.com/2007/11/04/magazine/04Flew-t.html.

8. This is the form of Darwin's statement in the first edition of *Origin of Species*, through the first six printings. As mentioned earlier, he added the words "breathed by the Creator" to subsequent editions, but regretted it ever after.

9. Richard Dawkins, *River Out of Eden: A Darwinian View of Life* (New York: Basic Books, 1995), 95–96, 131.

10. William B. Provine, "Scientists, Face It! Science and Religion are Incompatible," *Scientist* (Sept. 5, 1988):16, http://www.the-scientist.com/article/display/8667. (Subscription required.)

11. Thomas Malthus, *Essay on the Principle of Population; or, A View of Its Past and Present Effects on Human Happiness*, 7th ed. (New York: A. M. Kelley, 1971).

# NOTES

12. Charles Darwin, *The Descent of Man and Selection in Relation to Sex* (Franklin Center, PA: Franklin Library, 1980), 501.

13. Wiker, *The Myth of Darwin*, 66. (See chap. 2, n. 2.)

14. Ibid.

15. More than any one person, Sanger helped spawn the modern abortion industry. She frequently used the terms *human weeds* and *undesirables* with reference to those she deemed defective or unfit. She wrote in a 1925 essay, "Their lives are hopeless repetitions. . . . Such human weeds clog up the path, drain up the energies and the resources of this little earth. We must clear the way for a better world; we must cultivate our garden." Margaret Sanger, "The Need of Birth Control in America" in *Birth Control: Facts and Responsibilities,* ed. Adolf Meyer, MD (Baltimore: Williams and Wilkins Co., 1925), 11.

16. Randall K. O'Bannon, PhD, "Fifty Million Lost Lives Since 1973," *NRL News* 35, no. 1 (January 2008): 18, http://www.nrlc.org/news/2008/NRL01/LiveLost.html.

17. Michael White and John Gribbin, *Darwin: A Life in Science* (New York: Dutton Group, 1995), 156.

18. Robert G. Ingersoll, eulogy for his brother Ebon, delivered in Washington DC, May 31, 1879.

19. C. S. Lewis, *Surprised by Joy* (New York: Harcourt Brace, 1984), 21.

20. C. S. Lewis, *Mere Christianity* (New York: Macmillan, 1952), 45–46.

21. Genesis 3:17–18. See also Romans 8:19–22.

22. 1 Corinthians 15:19–22.

23. Psalm 19:1–4.

24. Acts 17:24–27.

25. Matthew 20:28.

26. David Berlinski, *The Devil's Delusion: Atheism and Its Scientific Pretensions* (New York: Basic Books, 2009), 187.

# NOTES

27. Charles H. Townes, "The Convergence of Science and Religion," *Think* 32, no. 2 (March-April 1966): 5.

28. Owen Gingerich, "Truth in Science: Proof, Persuasion, and the Galileo Affair," *Science & Christian Belief* 16, no. 1:25. http://www.scienceandchristianbelief.org/articles/Gingrich.pdf.

29. Ibid.

30. Quotations from Dr. Reeves and other recognized scientists at "Dissent from Darwin," http://www.dissentfromdarwin.org/scientists/.

31. Ibid.

32. Berlinski, "The Deniable Darwin," http://www.commentarymagazine.com/viewarticle.cfm/the-deniable-darwin-8573.

33. Darwin, *Origin of Species*, 492. (See chap. 1, n. 25.)

34. Ibid., 505.

35. Adapted from David Catchpoole, "Inside the Mind of a Killer: The Finnish high school tragedy once again shows that ideas have consequences," http://www.creation.com/inside-the-mind-of-a-killer.

36. G. R. Bozarth, "The Meaning of Evolution," *American Atheist* (September 20, 1979): 30.

# INDEX

167

# INDEX

# INDEX

# INDEX

# INDEX

## Share Your Thoughts

**With the Author:** Your comments will be forwarded to the author when you send them to *zauthor@zondervan.com*.

**With Zondervan:** Submit your review of this book by writing to *zreview@zondervan.com*.

## Free Online Resources at
## www.zondervan.com

**Zondervan AuthorTracker:** Be notified whenever your favorite authors publish new books, go on tour, or post an update about what's happening in their lives at www.zondervan.com/authortracker.

**Daily Bible Verses and Devotions:** Enrich your life with daily Bible verses or devotions that help you start every morning focused on God. Visit www.zondervan.com/newsletters.

**Free Email Publications:** Sign up for newsletters on Christian living, academic resources, church ministry, fiction, children's resources, and more. Visit www.zondervan.com/newsletters.

**Zondervan Bible Search:** Find and compare Bible passages in a variety of translations at www.zondervanbiblesearch.com.

**Other Benefits:** Register yourself to receive online benefits like coupons and special offers, or to participate in research.